Lindsay
ANDERSON

a guide to
references and resources

A
Reference
Guide
in
Film

Ronald Gottesman
Editor

Lindsay
ANDERSON

a guide to
references and resources

CHARLES L. P. SILET

G.K.HALL&CO.

70 LINCOLN STREET, BOSTON, MASS.

Library of Congress Cataloging in Publication Data
Silet, Charles L. P.
    Lindsay Anderson: a guide to references and
resources.

    (A reference publication in film)
    Bibliography: p.
    Includes index.
    1.   Anderson, Lindsay, 1923-   —Bibliography.
I.   Series.
Z8035.48.S54   [PN1998.A3]   016.79143′023′0924
ISBN 0-8161-8190-X   78-23208

This publication is printed on permanent/durable acid-free paper
MANUFACTURED IN THE UNITED STATES OF AMERICA

For Ronald Gottesman,
who has been teacher, mentor, friend

Contents

Preface

This book is primarily about Lindsay Anderson's career as a filmmaker and not about his equally distinguished careers as a film critic and a theater director. Obviously, his experience in these other two areas has had some influence on his films and in his approach to the making of films. Where this influence is apparent I have included sufficient materials to establish the connection. For example, "Lindsay Anderson: Critical Survey of Oeuvre," opens with a discussion of the more important of his critical articles on the art of the film because they form the background with which he went into filmmaking. Similar emphases exist in many of the other chapters, and perhaps a word on the guidelines I followed would be helpful to those who will be using this volume in order to study the film career of Lindsay Anderson.

"Lindsay Anderson: Biographical Background," and "Lindsay Anderson: Critical Survey of Oeuvre," contain my attempts to weave together his interests in film criticism and the theater with his career as a film director. The chapters are not burdened by cross references, but they do contain enough to suggest some interlocking of his activities. The initial chapter on Anderson's biographical background was examined by the director himself, and I am grateful for the care with which he went over the manuscript. He corrected a number of errors of fact as well as some of inference. The remaining infelicities in style are mine.

In the survey of the director's oeuvre, I have gathered together an overview of the most important themes and stylistic devices which characterize Anderson as an *auteur* of films. The relatively small number of major films which he has directed in his career has created some interesting leaps in style and often in theme. I have tried to suggest, however, that such leaps are consistent with his development as a filmmaker, and form traceable patterns within his film world.

The third chapter, "The Films: Synopses, Credits, and Notes," contains summaries of varying lengths, depending on the complexity and running time of the film. For his major films, *This Sporting Life, If . . ., O Lucky Man!,* and *In Celebration,* the synopses are quite long. Since he has directed so few major films and since those which he has directed are visually complex, I felt both the luxury and necessity of providing such extended descriptions. Most of his documentaries are unavailable for viewing in this country, and I had to rely on secondary sources for many of the synopses of those films. *The Singing Lesson* was available only from Poland, and was generously loaned to me through the Polish Embassy in Washington, D.C. It is unfortunate that *The White Bus* is distributed by United Artists only in Great Britain, and is therefore unavailable for viewing in this country.

The fourth chapter, "Annotated Guide to Writings," contains a variety of written items about Anderson's career as a filmmaker. First are those critical, often scholarly, articles which have assessed his films. Included in this category are many reviews published in both specialist film journals and in the popular press. There are necessarily more American items than British. I did not attempt to survey the provincial press in England for responses to Anderson's career in the same way that I did for American reactions outside New York. Also in this grouping are foreign language articles in French, German, Italian, Dutch, Czech, and Spanish, which demonstrate that Anderson has been received rather well critically on the Continent. I have listed interviews with Anderson in this section as well because such pieces are often subject to shaping beyond the control of the person being interviewed, and because I did not want them in the section which contained Anderson's own writings. A few of the items are reprints and were included to suggest that Anderson's reputation is broad enough and important enough for remarks about him and his films to receive fairly wide circulation. Finally, I have a select number of "letters to the editor" from readers of Anderson's critical writings which attest to the controversy often generated by his critical pronouncements and demonstrate that his critical writings did attract attention.

The section on "Performances, Writings, and Other Film Related Activity," contains a master list of Anderson's acting appearances, the awards he has received, his television work in both shows and commercials, and a complete catalog of the plays he has directed. Also included is a rather lengthy annotated bibliography of Anderson's critical writings. It is selective, however, since I omitted some of the materials that he wrote for the popular press. I have included a few of Anderson's "letters to the editor" which indicate the political nature of his position within the film community. The information on his plays and the list of commercials were supplied to me by Anderson himself, thereby making definitive what would have been incomplete if I had relied on other sources.

There is no archival source for the study of Lindsay Anderson. I have provided the address of the British Film Institute in this section because it contains more sources for researching him than any other specialized library would have. As I mentioned above, there are no distributors in the United States for either *The White Bus* or *The Singing Lesson*. I have listed, however, foreign distributors for both films. Otherwise, all other known sources of Anderson's films are incorporated in this chapter. The index is fairly comprehensive since I have supplied all references to books, films, and persons who appeared within the annotations. I included only the major figures from the film credits and the theater listings, as well as references to subjects such as the Cannes Film Festival. The index was designed to be as helpful as possible to the reader in his examination of Anderson's career.

Lindsay Anderson is a complex and talented man. His film work is only one of his areas of excellence. That he has achieved worldwide recognition in this highly competitive field based on such small output speaks well of his creative abilities. Some critics believe that he is the only British director who is worthy of such international acclaim. Anderson has earned a reputation as a tough-minded director who has not compromised his integrity. He has always made his position clear, and, in a world increasingly dominated by moral cowardice and ambivalence, that position is indeed refreshing. Lindsay Anderson is an unusual man, honest, gentle, and compassionate.

Mr. Anderson has been extraordinarily helpful in the making of this book. He has at all times answered my inquiries promptly and cheerfully. I wish to thank him publicly in this preface, as I have done many times privately, for his cooperation and patience.

A special acknowledgement is also due to Ronald Gottesman who has aided me in so many ways over the last 12 years, and to whom this volume is dedicated. Ron has provided me with numerous opportunities for professional advancement and guided my career in a variety of ways. This note can only inadequately suggest my gratitude for his kindness and understanding.

I should like to thank the following people and institutions that gave generously of both time and expertise: Nancy Brooker who furnished me with many good discussions about film; William Mischo, reference librarian at the Iowa State University Library, who did some valuable tracing of *Sequence* material; Sue Rusk, Martha Richardson, Cathy Murphy, Barbara Eichmeier, Elaine Campbell, Peggy Greisberger, and Susan Rafter of the Interlibrary Loan at the Iowa State University Library, who were enormously patient and resourceful in tracking down often obscure references; Don Pady, English librarian of the Iowa State University Library, who was once again cheerful and helpful with another of my projects; Donald R. Benson, chairman of the Department of English who gave me time off from my teaching duties when it was needed the most; Deans Wallace Russell and Nathan Dean of the College of Science and Humanities who provided research funds; and Vice President Daniel Zaffarano of the Graduate College who generously paid for research assistance, duplication, and typing.

The following people provided me with information about Anderson's films: Peter Seward and Linda Wood of the British Film Institute, London;

Gloria Sachs, Films Officer of the Ministry of Agriculture, Fisheries, and Foods, London; Francis Gysin, Films Officer, National Coal Board, London; R. A. Hardy of the National Society for the Prevention of Cruelty to Children, London; Larry Kardish of the Museum of Modern Art, New York; M. Romaniuk, Information Officer of the Embassy of the Polish People's Republic, Washington, D. C.; S. A. Windus, Film Production Librarian, Central Office of Information, London.

There are three individuals to whom I owe a special debt of gratitude: Barbara Garrey of G. K. Hall & Co. for her tolerance of my sliding deadlines; Zora Devrnja Zimmerman for dealing with a mountain of translating with good humor; and Deborah Fitzgerald, my research assistant, for her tireless commitment to the project.

Finally, to my children, Kris, Scott, Karin, and Emily, for their patience while the book was underfoot and they were not, and to Kay for her loving support and understanding at all stages of this project, I give my heartfelt thanks.

Biographical Background

With the exception of a painter who was a "a bit mad and a bit drunk," Lindsay Gordon Anderson does not think that his Scottish ancestors were a particularly creative lot. [1] He suspects that the fact that he is three-quarters Scot, however, accounts for his moral intransigence as well as his distance from the English traditions in both theater and cinema. His father, Major General A. V. Anderson, was from Stonehaven, Scotland, and his mother, Estelle Bell Gasson, although from Queenstown, South Africa, was the daughter of an English wool merchant who married a girl of Scottish background. The Andersons have been a military family for several generations. In fact, his father was stationed as a captain in Bangalore, India, with the Royal Engineers when Lindsay Gordon was born in 1923.

When Anderson was still quite young, he returned to the south of England with his mother. His parents were divorced when he was ten, and his mother married again soon afterwards. In England Anderson received a conventional upper middle-class education. He attended a preparatory school, St. Ronan's in Worthing, and public school at Cheltenham College. Later he returned briefly to Cheltenham for the setting of his most famous film, *If...* In 1941 Anderson read classics for a year at Wadham College, Oxford, while he was taking his pre-officer training as a volunteer in the army, an action prompted by the war.

Anderson is the middle child of three boys. His older brother was commissioned into the Royal Tank Regiment shortly before the Second World War, but spent most of the war flying for the Royal Air Force. His younger brother was commissioned into the navy and died while in peacetime service in the Pacific. Lindsay served in the 60th King's Royal Rifle Groups and the Intelligence Corps from 1943 to 1946. Returning to Oxford in 1946, he switched his academic major to English, finally taking a master of arts degree in 1948. While at school, he acted in plays: an Oxford University Dramatic Society production, two dramas produced by Kenneth Tynan, and one drama with Guy Brenton, with whom he was later to make *Thursday's Children.* He really did not enjoy the atmosphere of amateur dramatics at Oxford. He later recalled to Elizabeth Sussex that they were

1

"very pseudo-professional and very competitive in a rather unpleasant way."[2]

Classic and foreign language films were difficult to see during the war, and he did not receive much exposure to any at Cheltenham, although he does remember seeing *Citizen Kane* there. So it was with a great sense of discovery that he saw John Ford's *My Darling Clementine* at the Odeon, Leicester Square, a year after the war. It was his first real creative shock in the cinema. Anderson had been viewing films "on strictly a fan level" for years, but with the founding of *Sequence,* the magazine of the Oxford University Film Society, he turned professional. *Sequence 1* was the beginning number of what was to become a highly influential journal. It was influential not only because of the content of the articles it published, but also because it provided such a fertile training ground for young British film critics and filmmakers. The film society had already published a single issue of a journal called the *Film Society Magazine* before Anderson returned to Oxford. In the hands of Anderson and Peter Ericsson, and later Penelope Houston, Gavin Lambert, and Karel Reisz, *Sequence* was transformed from an undergraduate film society bulletin into a journal of international significance. The magazine was published from 1946 to 1952, 14 issues total, and survived a move from Oxford to London after the editors graduated.

To the initial issue *Sequence 1* (December 1946), edited by Peter Ericsson and John Boud, Anderson contributed his first essay. It discussed contemporary French films, the result of a recent trip to Paris. The second number which appeared in the winter of 1947 had a different format. This time the issue was edited by Anderson and Penelope Houston as well as Ericsson. Gavin Lambert, a school friend of Anderson who was then in London, contributed a piece on British cinema while Ericsson wrote a long article on John Ford. The cover bore a still from Ford's *My Darling Clementine.* The thrust of the journal from the beginning was a reaction against the critical inflation then accorded to British films. The editors wanted to draw attention to the lively and dynamic filmmaking in America. They also discovered new Continental directors as well as filmmakers of the past.

In 1958 Anderson revealed that "at the beginning, though, *Sequence* was more concerned with the rediscovery and reaffirmation of the poetic quality of the cinema (I prefer the word poetic to aesthetic) than with fighting the immediate practical battle of getting films made."[3] Gavin Lambert, who was one of the editors from the third issue onward, later remembered the days of *Sequence* as a period of self-discovery for the editors.

> We were never theorists, and we had few 'principles.' As each number
> was written and published, we found out what we were about. All we
> basically knew was that we cared about personal films, not official ideas
> about 'art,' and *Sequence* was partly a series of love letters to directors we
> admired, partly a succession of hate-mail against work we despised.[4]

Anderson published a number of essays in which he set forth his critical and artistic credo. "Angles of Approach" (*see* no. 357), "Creative Elements" (*see* no. 360), and "The Director's Cinema?" (*see* no. 372), were all published in *Sequence.* These early articles not only established Anderson as a critic of decidedly personal views, but also suggested the direction he would later take as a director. He wrote reviews of the films of John Ford and argued against the stodginess of the British film industry. Anderson covered the Cannes Film Festival for the journal as he did later for *Sight and Sound,* and for non-specialist papers like *The Times,* the *Observer,* and *The New Statesman.*

By 1948 the editors moved to London and took the magazine with them. The editors continued to write most of the copy, often supplying *noms de plume* from the films they had seen. For example, they used the names Alberta Marlow, the Mary Astor character from *The Maltese Falcon,* and Adam Helmer from *Drums Along the Mohawk.* It was the famous cover still from *She Wore a Yellow Ribbon* of John Wayne leading his horse which prompted Samuel Goldwyn in his interview with Anderson to give advice on how to increase the circulation of *Sequence:* "Get a pretty girl on the cover. Look at this—just a horse. Who cares about horses?"[5] (*see* no. 377). Most of the later issues were edited by Anderson, Ericsson, who now worked at the Foreign Office, and Gavin Lambert, who was writing scripts for commercials. Anderson was the only editor who worked on the entire run of the magazine. The final issue, New Year's 1952, was edited by Anderson and Karel Reisz, whom he had met quite accidentally at the National Film Archive. Their meeting was to prove fruitful for both men.

Anderson's first opportunity to make a film came in 1948. The Oxford University Film Society had hosted the annual meeting of the Federation of Film Societies in 1947, and among the people Anderson met was Lois Sutcliffe, wife of the managing director of a Yorkshire-based conveyor belt manufacturing firm, Richard Sutcliffe, Ltd. When the firm began searching for a director to make a documentary about conveyor belts, Lois Sutcliffe remembered Anderson from their Oxford meeting. After two London film companies that they had approached submitted disappointing scripts, she told her husband about Anderson, and on her recommendation he was hired.

Meet the Pioneers was shot in 1948 with a surplus Air Force camera by the local school master, John Jones, with the help of Edward Brendon who was working as an assistant director on features at British National. Anderson recalled that he knew nothing about making films and that he learned as they went along. He had agreed to have the film ready to show at a mining machinery exhibition. Unfortunately, he allowed only two days for editing the 40-minute film. "I imagined that the editing of a film was simply the joining together of shots in an order that one already knew before-hand."[6] He did the cutting without stopping in about 72 hours in order to make the show. Anderson himself read the commentary and arranged the music (from Aaron Copeland to Smetana) from phonograph records. The film satisfied the Sutcliffes, and they asked him to make another. Unfortunately, the next venture had to be abandoned because the camera kept jamming.

For *Idlers That Work* in 1949, the Sutcliffes bought a new camera and hired a new cameraman, George Levy, a camera assistant working at Ealing Studios, since Jones had moved away from Wakefield. The third Sutcliffe film, *Three Installations,* was made in 1952. The film was especially important for Anderson because it brought him together with Walter Lassally who worked as the cameraman and with whom Anderson would work later. Derek York, who was the editor for the film, had formed an amateur unit with Lassally called Screencraft, and they had just completed their film about squatters called *Smith Our Friend.*

Anderson made his last film for the Sutcliffes, *Trunk Conveyor,* in 1952. Since Lassally was previously engaged, he used as his camerman John Reid, who had worked for the coal board before. The film was made almost entirely in the pit using the required safety lighting.

On the recommendation of the Sutcliffes, Anderson was commissioned to make a documentary about a newspaper, *The Wakefield Express* (1952), for the paper's 100th anniversary. He used Lassally as cameraman. John Fletcher, who used to help out with *Sequence,* recorded the school children and the band and helped with the editing.

In 1953 Anderson joined a friend from Oxford to make *Thursday's Children.* Guy Brenton, then an assistant with BBC television, had visited the Royal School for the Deaf at Margate. He was so impressed by it that he invited Anderson to work with him on a film about the school which the two would finance with their own money. Walter Lassally again provided the camera work and Richard Burton agreed to narrate. Eventually, World Wide Pictures furnished them with the money to complete the project. The film won a Hollywood Oscar award and was booked on the Granada chain in Britain, but was never given major distribution. While editing the film, Anderson, who was not at that time a member of the cinema technicians union, ran afoul of the World Wide Studios shop steward. He was told he could be in the room where the editing was going on but could not touch the film, an order which ceased to be effective the moment the shop steward left the room. He made two or three applications before he was finally admitted to the trade union. Some left-wing members of the union felt that since Anderson had a university degree there was nothing to prevent him from earning his living as a schoolmaster. *O Dreamland,* also made in 1953, was Anderson's project alone. While making *Thursday's Children,* he discovered an amusement park called Dreamland, and with only one assistant, John Fletcher, acting as cameraman, he made a documentary about the park. Initially he made the film just for his own amusement, never really expecting that it would be shown publicly. But in 1956 it was shown at the National Film Theater as part of the first Free Cinema program.

In 1952, while Anderson was editing *Three Installations* in the cutting room of Leon Clore, he met Clore's future wife, Miriam, who had arrived from Israel to learn film editing. She was assigned to a cutting room next to Anderson's but union regulations would not allow her to do anything. Anderson invited her to watch him. "I said she could come into my cutting room and carry the cans about. She came and did little odd jobs, and I taught her how to make joins."[7] This was how Anderson met Leon Clore. During 1955 Clore produced seven short films which Anderson shot for various sponsoring agencies. The first films were four five-minute trailers for the National Society for the Prevention of Cruelty to Children (NSPCC). Anderson scripted all the films and Walter Lassally photographed them. The films were little dramas to show how children are mistreated. In *Henry,* Anderson used one of the small boys he had used in the chorus in *Green and Pleasant Land,* and in this same film he played the NSPCC officer who finally comes to rescue Henry. This was the first film to use the new fast stock, Ilford H.P.S., a necessity since the film was shot entirely at night without additional lighting. This same year Anderson also made two informational films for the National Industrial Fuel Efficiency Service, *Twenty Pounds a Ton* and *Energy First.* These five-minute films were shot by cameraman Larry Pizer, with John Fletcher acting as production manager. Anderson finished the year with a 20-minute informational film on hoof-and-mouth disease for the Central Office of Information for the Ministry of Agriculture called *Foot and Mouth.* Anderson narrated and Lassally was his camerman.

In addition to these documentaries, Anderson organized a John Ford festival at the National Film Theater. In 1955 he also directed his first episode for the Robin Hood television series, called "Secret Mission". He edited Lorenza Mazzetti's film, *Together,* her poetic story of two deaf mutes in the East End of London. Walter Lassally did some extra shooting. John Fletcher helped, and Leon Clore provided the cutting room. The film was later shown along with *O Dreamland* in the first program of the Free Cinema series. Anderson was also commissioned to write a monograph on John Ford by Gavin Lambert who was then editor of *Sight and Sound.* The study was finished by the end of 1955 but by then Lambert had left the editorship of the journal and the project was dropped because of lack of funds. Anderson's monograph on Ford was finally published in the magazine *Cinema* in 1971 (*see* no. 434).

In 1956 Anderson continued to direct material for the Robin Hood series, working on four episodes: "The Imposters," "Ambush," "The Haunted Mill," and "Isabella." An unknown young actor, John Schlesinger, played the part of the baker in the episode "The Haunted Mill." The important event in Anderson's film career in 1956 was not, however, the production of these television episodes, but rather the program of the first Free Cinema films at the National Film Theater, which he helped organize. Anderson recalls that he had coined the term "Free Cinema" quite by accident a number of years before by adding a brief statement to an article by Alan Cooke on American avant-garde films for *Sequence*. He wrote the phrase "Free Cinema" into the last paragraph and titled the piece "Free Cinema" as well. "We were always rewriting people's things," he recalled later of the *Sequence* days.[8] There were six programs in the series presented at the National Film Theater, of which only three contained films made in Britain. The others included films by Franju (*Le Sang des Bêtes*), Rogosin (*On the Bowery*), Polanski (*Two Men and a Wardrobe*), Truffaut (*Les Mistons*), and Chabrol (*Le Beau Serge*). Five of the 11 British films were sponsored by the British Film Institute's Experimental Film Fund, and two of the films were made with money from the Ford Motor Company.

The first of the Ford Motor Company-sponsored films was Anderson's *Every Day Except Christmas* made in 1957. The film's genesis came from Karel Reisz, who had taken a job with Ford Motor Company making advertising films on the condition that he be allowed to produce a series of documentaries which did not have any relationship with the company. He asked Anderson to make the first film. Anderson had recently been approached by the BBC to direct a film about long-distance truck drivers but the project had fallen through. His first thought was to tie together the idea of truck drivers with hauling the fishing catch from all over Britain, making a rather epic and dramatic story of the long-distance drivers. Finally Anderson decided to do a film on Covent Garden. He was asked to do further work on the Robin Hood series but Reisz insisted that he first undertake the documentary. The film was improvised on location except for a brief outline Anderson drew up after observing the activities in the market. It took him five months to edit the initial footage.

While Anderson was making his early documentaries, he continued to write film criticism as well. Before the collapse of *Sequence*, he had already begun writing articles and reviews for *Sight and Sound*, and, when the former magazine ceased publication altogether, Anderson merely moved over to *Sight and Sound*. He completed more reviews of Cannes, wrote about Humphrey Jennings, reviewed the later films of John Ford, and began to survey French film criticism by reviewing French film journals. He was also generous in his reviews of low-budget, experimental films, usually by unknown filmmakers. He was especially struck by their freshness of approach which compensated for their technical inexperience. Several of his *Sight and Sound* articles created quite a stir, especially his analysis of the ending of *On the Waterfront* (*see* no. 403). Then, as now, Anderson did not shy away from controversy. In such pieces as "Stand Up! Stand Up!" (*see* no. 414) and "Get Out and Push" (*see* no. 421), he tried once again to stimulate critical thinking about films.

In 1952 Anderson wrote the book *Making a Film: The Story of 'Secret People'* (*see* no. 381), which was a study of the construction of Thorold Dickinson's film.

It is a fascinating piece of work because Anderson traces the entire history of the film from its beginnings through the final editing. Writing the book must have been excellent training for someone who would later make feature films of his own. By the end of the fifties, however, Anderson was turning more of his energies to the theater and to his political or social involvement. His writings on film fell rapidly after 1958. He has written little of a critical nature since then.

In 1958, because of his connections with the *Universities and Left Review* and the New Left movement, Anderson became involved with the production of a documentary of the first Easter march of the Campaign for Nuclear Disarmament to the atomic weapons plant in Aldermaston. The film did not originate from the Free Cinema movement but was an idea of Derrick Knight and a committee of 11 consisting of Anderson, Christopher Bruñel, Charles Cooper, Allan Forbes, Kurt Lewenhack, Lewis McLeod, Kârel Reisz, Elizabeth Russell, Eda Segal, and Derek York. The film was directed by a number of committee members, among them Anderson. He made his biggest contribution, however, when he took over the editing, which he did with Mary Beale. The final version of the commentary was also Anderson's, although Christopher Logue did some of it, and, at Anderson's behest, Richard Burton delivered it.

The film was made from stock collected from the junk rooms of Pinewood Studios, or what the filmmakers could obtain from people like Leon Clore. Large numbers of people from the film industry worked long hours for free on this film. The experience was truly a communal one.

In spite of the fact that *Thursday's Children* was distributed after it won a Hollywood Oscar in 1955, Anderson's film work began to diminish. A number of projects fell through, either because the sponsors withdrew or because Anderson did not feel the freedom to work with them. Even *Every Day Except Christmas* was first turned down by the British selection committee for submission to the Venice Film Festival. It finally won the Grand Prix in spite of the disapproval of the representatives of the British filmmakers' association because, in their opinion, it gave an unflattering view of British life. Anderson's problems with the industry continued after *Every Day Except Christmas*. Ealing Studios offered him the chance to do a feature, and he suggested making a film from a book about the emergency ward of a hospital based on Robert Lowry's novel *Casualty*. After a few weeks of observing the emergency facilities at Guy's Hospital, Anderson drafted a preliminary idea for the film. The studio wanted more romantic materials in the film than Anderson felt competent to draft, but when he suggested that they find a writer to work with him on the script, they refused. He realized later that they were not terribly interested in pursuing the project.

In 1959 Anderson went to the Royal Court Theater to direct Willis Hall's play "The Long and The Short and The Tall". He had previously directed Kathleen Sull's "The Waiting for Lester Abbs" in one of the Sunday night productions for the English Stage Company in 1957 at the invitation of Tony Richardson. The success of his production of Hall's play earned him an invitation to direct more plays for the Royal Court, and over the next few years he did Alun Owen's "Progress to the Park" and John Arden's "Serjeant Musgrave's Dance" in 1959; Harry Cookson's "The Lily White Boys", Keith Waterhouse and Willis Hall's "Billy Liar", and Christopher Logue's "Trials by Logue" in 1960; and Max Frisch's "The Fire Raisers" in 1961. Despite his success in the theater, his film career did not flourish during these years. When Ealing Studios decided to make a film of "The Long and The Short and The Tall," they did not ask Anderson to direct it. They felt that he had not had enough film experience to manage a feature film. It should be noted that they also did not think that Peter O'Toole, who had played the lead in the stage version, was strong enough to play the part in the film.

The popular success of *Saturday Night and Sunday Morning* changed the complexion of the British film industry enough to accommodate Anderson. The domination of the industry by middleclass films was seriously challenged by Jack Clayton's *Room at the Top* in 1958. It was Karel Reisz and Tony Richardson and Woodfall Films, however, that really capitalized on that breakthrough with *Saturday Night and Sunday Morning,* and provided the climate which finally allowed Anderson to make his first feature film.

David Storey's novel, *This Sporting Life,* initially appeared in 1960 and, although Anderson was one of the first people to think about filming the book, it was Karel Reisz who provided him with the opportunity. The film rights were bought by the Rank organization for Julian Wintle and Leslie Parkyn of Independent Artists after Woodfall's attempts to purchase them failed through lack of money. Wintle and Parkyn wanted Reisz to direct the film, but Reisz wanted, instead, to gain some experience in producing, and he suggested that Anderson should be the one to direct *This Sporting Life (see no. 16).* This was the beginning of a long and fruitful collaboration between Storey and Anderson which continues to this day.

Anderson wrote that he was originally attracted by the vividness and immediacy of the writing in Storey's novel, which had a "sense of poetry dark, passionate and wholly his own." It was this sense which Anderson wanted to capture in his film version of the novel. The first script Storey produced, after detailed discussions with Anderson and Reisz, lacked much of the spirit of the book. Meanwhile, they had interested Richard Harris in the lead part of Frank Machin and mailed him a copy of the script. After they did not hear from him, Anderson flew to Tahiti where Harris was filming *Mutiny on the Bounty* to consult with him about the part. Harris finally convinced Anderson that the essence of the novel had been lost in the script, and the two men discussed the reconstruction of the screenplay. After each day's shooting of *Mutiny,* Harris and Anderson met in his bungalow and went through the script and the heavily annotated version of the novel

Harris had. Anderson returned to London with his notes and Storey agreed to reshape the screenplay.

The film is set in the north of England, and in searching for the proper shooting location, Anderson discovered that Storey had grown up about ten minutes away from the Sutcliffe factory in Yorkshire when Anderson was making his first films for that firm. In the filming of *This Sporting Life* Anderson was able to use his knowledge of the north of England which had appeared in his documentaries, and finally brought to fruition his imaginative conception of that part of the country[9]

While Anderson was making *This Sporting Life,* he and Harris decided to do a remake of *Wuthering Heights.* The project fell through after much work when Harris went to Hollywood. In 1963, however, Anderson did direct Harris' solo performance at the Royal Court in an adaptation they had made of Gogol's "The Diary of a Madman." After *This Sporting Life,* Anderson went back to the theater, first by accepting an invitation to direct Max Frisch's "Andorra" with Tom Courtenay at the National Theater, and then by assuming the joint artistic directionship with Anthony Page of the Royal Court for the 1964-1965 season. He directed Shakespeare's "Julius Caesar" in 1964. He also began directing commercials at this time, which he prefers for work when he needs money over directing feature films in which he does not believe. In 1963, for example, Anderson directed two commercials for Fry's Picnic, 17 for Mackeson, one for Persil, and six for Rowntree. In 1964 he shot two for Horlicks, 13 for Mackeson, and five for Rowntree. In 1965 he did seven more for Mackeson, two for Ronson Razor, and two for Whitbread Tankard. He made only one commercial in 1967 for Alcan, and five in 1968, one for Black Magic and four for Kraft C/B.[10]

In 1965 Anderson gained his second opportunity to direct a fiction film. Oscar Lewenstein, producing for Woodfall, suggested that each of the Free Cinema directors, Reisz, Richardson, and Anderson, should contribute one segment to a film trilogy of independent subjects. Reisz withdrew when he realized that his film, *A Suitable Case for Treatment* (later *Morgan*), would run to feature length, and he was replaced by Peter Brook. Richardson wanted to film the Shelagh Delaney short story, "Pavan for a Dead Princess," which provided Lewenstein with the idea that all three segments should be based on stories by Delaney. Anderson was offered "The White Bus" from her collection *Sweetly Sings the Donkey* (*see* no. 70). After seeing Anderson's completed picture, however, the other two directors embarked on other subjects. Brook directed Zero Mostel in *The Ride of the Valkyries* and Richardson made a film, *Red and Blue,* based on a number of songs and starring Venessa Redgrave. The final trilogy, which Anderson titled *Red, White and Zero,* lacked coherence, and United Artists shelved it. Finally, the individual segments achieved a few scattered showings as "short subjects." *The White Bus* was shown once commercially in a South Kensington cinema on a double bill with *Daisies* by Vera Chytilova. The Czech film was violently attacked by the critics, and *The White Bus* received very little notice. The program was quickly withdrawn. By then Anderson was already shooting *If....*

In 1966 Anderson was invited to direct "The Cherry Orchard" starring Tom Courtenay and Celia Johnson at the Chichester Festival Theater. He also went to Warsaw to direct Tadeusz Lomnicki in "Inadmissible Evidence" by John Osborne at the Contemporary Theater. Anderson had first seen Lomnicki in *A Generation* at the Cannes Film Festival in 1957. He later met the young Polish actor on a trip he made to Poland for BBC television. For several years Lomnicki thought that Anderson would come to Warsaw to direct him in "Hamlet." This idea was scrapped in favor of a contemporary play. While in Warsaw, however, Anderson made another film, this time on invitation from the Warsaw Documentary Studios. The subject was suggested through Anderson's assistant at the theater who also worked with a seasoned musical comedy actor, Professor Ludwik Sempolinski, at the Warsaw Dramatic Academy. The assistant brought Anderson to one of the professor's classes in "Song Presentation," with the third-year dramatic students. During the class, he heard three of the songs which were eventually included in *The Singing Lesson (Raz Dwa Trzy)*. Anderson employed a young Polish cameraman, Zygmunt Samosiuk, who spoke very little English but who worked well with Anderson. The film was finished in 1967 and, like *The White Bus,* has never played commercially in the United States. Both films were shown in 1973 at a retrospective of Anderson's films at the Pacific Film Archive, University Art Museum, Berkeley, California.

If... began to take shape before *The Singing Lesson* was even started. Anderson was introduced to the original idea in September 1966 by Seth Holt who wanted to produce it at the time. The original story, *Crusaders,* was the product of two young men, John Howlett and David Sherwin, who had attended public school together in 1958 and had completed the initial draft of the script by 1960. By the time Anderson became involved with the property, Howlett was in Rome working with Holt on another project and it was Sherwin who redrafted the script with Anderson. Both Sherwin and Anderson worked on the screenplay during most of 1967. The ending was changed from the suicide of the hero to his open rebellion. Other alterations made by Anderson also put a good deal of himself into the film. Later, when shooting, Anderson used his old school, Cheltenham College, for the exteriors. Holt backed out as producer when he became too embroiled in directing his own films, so Michael Medwin, who was head of Memorial Enterprises, the company founded by Albert Finney, took over. The people at Memorial were enthusiastic about the idea but funding was difficult to obtain. The script was rejected by almost every British distributor. The American television company CBS accepted the project as their first feature film production, but withdrew six weeks before shooting was due to begin. *If...* was finally rescued by Charles Bludhorn of Paramount.

The filming began in March of 1968 with a budget of £250,000. The modesty of the budget was a factor in one of the film's most controversial features, the shifting back and forth from color to black and white. The monochrome sequences were prompted originally by the need to conserve money; the aesthetic was thus inspired by economics. Anderson was rather hesitant about shooting in color, and relied heavily on Jocelyn Herbert, the designer with whom he had worked at the Royal Court, and Miroslav Ondricek, who had been the camerman on *The White Bus*. The film was shot in ten weeks with a minimum of over-shooting from a tightly constructed script. The on-the-screen camera movements and angles were worked out on the set. David Gladwell, in an article (*see* no. 125), described his working relationship with Anderson. It was made clear to Gladwell that Anderson would be editing the film, and that Gladwell was expected to follow the script in cutting. The film's release coincided with the rising tide of student violence, especially in the United States. The timeliness of the movie helped to increase Anderson's stature as a popular filmmaker, but confused the critics who often accused Anderson of pandering to youth with trendy films.

The critical reception which *If...* received both in Great Britain and abroad, especially in the United States, helped to secure Anderson's reputation as a film director of international recognition. The packaging of the film for distribution in the United States alienated a few of the American critics who felt that the publicity was clearly aimed at capitalizing on the current campus violence and the youth-oriented audience. The presence of the campus riots inevitably suggested comparisons with the film, but Anderson feels that the criticism levelled at Paramount's advertising campaign because of this was grossly unfair. In fact, he found that most American critics approached the film with far more seriousness and perception than the British critics did.

The film's international reception was generally enthusiastic and Anderson won another prize at the Cannes Film Festival, this time the Grand Prix. However, the violent and socially critical qualities of *If...* resulted in its censorship or suppression in many parts of the world. Generally, it was highly successful in Europe, although at first Italy attempted to ban it (a decision reversed only by vehement critical protest). The film could not be shown in Spain, and was severely truncated in then-fascist Greece. Poland accepted the film in a festival of British cinema, but refused to distribute it properly; South Africa subjected it to numerous puritanical cuts. Clearly, the film was, both in content and as an object, dealing with contemporary political realities. When *State of Siege*, a political film by Costa-Gavras, was deleted from the opening season of the American Film Institute's new theater, Anderson withdrew *If...* in protest to the censorship. The film continues to elicit strong opinions from those who see it.[11]

Amid all the uproar about *If...*, Anderson's next film, *O Lucky Man!* (*see* no. 20), began to gestate. David Sherwin says that the script was begun on the publicity tour of America which he and Malcolm McDowell took to promote *If...* (*see* no. 232). While in New York for the opening, Sherwin told McDowell about his idea for a story called *Manpower*, about an out-of-work young man who starts at the bottom and works his way up the economic ladder. McDowell told Sherwin about the story he had been contemplating since he finished *If....* It was called *Coffee Man* and concerned a young coffee salesman trainee who is suddenly and without adequate training sent to Yorkshire to replace a salesman who vanished without notice. The treatment was highly autobiographical since McDowell drew heavily on his own experience as a coffee salesman trainee and on his subsequent acting career. Sherwin dropped his *Manpower* idea at McDowell's suggestion and began work on *Coffee Man.* By January 1970, about a year later, Sherwin had typed the first 20 pages or so of the script, which takes the hero through the coffee sampling section, and had shown it to Anderson who thought it was too naturalistic and too sketchy but encouraged Sherwin and McDowell to keep working on it. By August of the same year, they had added the key ingredient, luck, to the story and had retitled it *Lucky Man.* In a meeting with Anderson in that same month, the director suggested, as inspirations, Kafka's *Amerika* and Bunyan's *Pilgrim's Progress,* plus a bit of Candide. Anderson changed the title to *O Lucky Man!*.

The film did not have any financial backing other than modest sums from Anderson and McDowell plus Sherwin's talent as a script writer, but they went ahead with the preparation of a script in the same way that they had with *If....* Sherwin noted that they felt freer that way to develop the idea in any way they could. After the script was completed, they could go to a producer for the backing to shoot it.

In February 1971, Anderson contacted Alan Price about performing songs for the film. Anderson had planned to do a documentary about Price at one time, but ran into difficulties over copyright material. A record company wanted to charge £1000 a minute for a Ray Charles number, so the project was abandoned. Anderson, however, had not forgotten the music which Price had written for David Storey's play, "Home", which he directed in 1970 at the Royal Court, and he wanted Price to do the music for *O Lucky Man!*. After he had written "My Home Town," "Poor People," "Everyone's Going Through Changes," "O Lucky Man," and "Sell, Sell, Sell," Anderson remarked wryly that the songs would save the film.

By October 1971, the first draft of the script was completed, but only after long and agonizing sessions between Storey and Anderson. Again they took it to Michael Medwin to produce. Anderson assembled much of his old crew from *If....* He had to make a special trip to Czechoslovakia to obtain permission for Miroslav Ondricek, who had shot *If...*, to come to England for *O Lucky Man!*. On December 24, Sherwin received a postcard from Anderson who was in New York. Warner Brothers had agreed to finance the film at $1.5 million. The work on the script continued until shooting actually began on March 20, 1972.[12]

While all of the preparations for *O Lucky Man!* were being made, Anderson was directing plays and shooting commercials. In 1969 he did five for Campari, two for Guiness Stout, and 17 for Kelloggs. In 1970 he shot three for Findus, and in 1971, one for Alcan and one for Presige Ewbank. Anderson was also busy directing plays. After a three-year break from theater work, he directed David Storey's play, "In Celebration," at the Royal Court in 1969 (in 1975 he made a film version for the American Film Theater series). In the same year he also directed Storey's next play, "The Contractor." In rapid succession Anderson directed four more of Storey's plays: "Home" in 1970, "The Changing Room" in 1971, "The Farm" in 1973, and "Life Class" in 1974. Of these, only "Home" came to New York in its original production, with its original cast headed by Sir John Gielgud and Sir Ralph Richardson. This production was eventually taped for educational television distribution by New York's WNET. It was another of Anderson's projects for which British financing could not be obtained.

Also in 1969, Anderson was named to the Board of Governors of the British Film Institute. He resigned from that position the next year in protest against slothful and reactionary politics. He was named the Director of the Year by the British publication, *T.V. Mail*, and the following year received the same honor from the *International Film Guide*. John Fletcher made a short film which was released in 1969 about the making of *The White Bus*. Fletcher, who had worked with Anderson on *Thursday's Children* and *Every Day Except Christmas*, shot this documentary about Anderson as he directed *The White Bus*. It took Fletcher and his wife three years to edit the film, *About The White Bus* (*see* no. 350), which has been seen more frequently than the original film itself.

In 1974 Anderson directed the film version of Storey's "In Celebration" for the American Film Theater. He used the original cast from his Royal Court production of 1969. The film was one of the most highly acclaimed of the series. In 1975 Anderson was directing plays and did three that year: Joe Orton's "What the Butler Saw" at the Royal Court; his own adaptation of Anton Chekhov's "The Sea Gull" with his own company at the Lyric Theater, London; and a comedy hit, "The Bed Before Yesterday" by the veteran author Ben Travers. In 1977 Anderson directed William Douglas Home's "The Kingfisher," once again at the Lyric Theater.

In 1973 the Pacific Film Archive at the University Art Museum in Berkeley, California, held a three day retrospective of Anderson's films. It was the largest single showing of his films in the United States. The films screened were *Thursday's Children, O Dreamland, The Singing Lesson, This Sporting*

Life, The White Bus, If . . ., and *O Lucky Man!.* Anderson was also the featured director at the National Film Theatre in August, 1977, when, as British Cinema Part 3, the largest retrospective ever shown of his films was mounted. The following films were shown: *Wakefield Express; Thursday's Children; Together; March to Aldermaston; O Dreamland; Every Day Except Christmas; The White Bus; The Singing Lesson; This Sporting Life; If . . .; O Lucky Man!;* and *In Celebration.*

Anderson's career both in the theater and in film has exhibited a refreshing individuality. He has consistently refused to become tied to either the film establishment or the theater establishment here or in England. He has preferred to make commercials when he needs money since they are relatively easy to make and do not require any great outlay of energy. He has chosen his film properties with care, and to date, he has directed only four major commercial films, one of which was a filmed drama. At the present time, he continues to experiment with the medium and to extend the possibilities of the film experience.

NOTES

1. The study of Anderson by Elizabeth Sussex in 1969 provided me with a good deal of the biographical information contained in this chapter. For further reference, *see* Elizabeth Sussex, *Lindsay Anderson* (New York: Frederick A. Praeger, 1969).

2. Sussex, *Lindsay Anderson,* p. 9

3. "The Critical Issue: A Discussion Between Paul Rotha, Basil Wright, Lindsay Anderson, Penelope Houston," *Sight and Sound,* 27 (Autumn 1958), 274.

4. Gavin Lambert, Introduction to Lindsay Anderson's "John Ford," *Cinema,* 6 (Spring 1971), 22.

5. "Goldwyn at Claridges," *Sequence,* 13 (New Year 1951), 10.

6. Sussex, *Lindsay Anderson,* p. 15.

7. Ibid., p. 26

8. *Ibid.,* p. 30.

9. Anderson has written of his experiences getting *This Sporting Life* together in his article "Sport, Life, and Art," *Films and Filming,* 9 (February 1963), 15-18.

10. Lindsay Anderson supplied me with the information on his commercials.

11. Anderson supplied an introduction to the screenplay of *If . . .* which was published. See *If . . .: A Film by Lindsay Anderson and David Sherwin* (New York: Simon and Schuster, 1969).

12. *For a further discussion of Anderson's preparations for O Lucky Man!,* see his "Preface," Lindsay Anderson and David Sherwin with Songs by Alan Price, *O Lucky Man!* (New York: Grove Press, 1973), and Lindsay Anderson, " Stripping the Veils Away," the *Times,* (London)(21 April 1973), p. 17.

Critical Survey of Oeuvre

I

In 1956, after completing his work on the Robin Hood television series, Anderson wrote a short piece for *Sight and Sound* discussing that experience. "Notes from Sherwood" is confessional because Anderson admits that he did not really understand the pressures which were faced by commercial directors who must meet deadlines and budgets on a week-to-week basis. Neither his training in documentary film nor his background as a critic prepared him for working in a studio. What fascinated Anderson about the experience was watching all of "one's own clichés came to life." "Film-making *is* a compound of 'Creative Elements,'" he wrote; "also it *is* the director's medium—provided that the writer has given him the material to work with in the first place."[1] Anderson's attitudes toward film clearly reflect his training as a film critic, an activity which he pursued for over ten years. During that period he had ample time to formulate his views on films and filmmakers.

The search for the origins of Lindsay Anderson's film career must begin in the pages of *Sequence,* that brash and uncompromising publication which started life as the magazine of the Oxford University Film Society. His early training was not in hauling props or assisting the cameraman on a studio backlot, but rather it was in observing with a critical eye and a sharp pen the world of the film. Unlike most American and British directors, Anderson was not trained in the guild system of the film industry. His background was much more like that of the Continental directors who received their apprenticeship writing movie criticism for *Cahiers du Cinéma* under the tutelage of Andre Bazin. Anderson, like the "New Wave" directors, learned to observe films first and to make them later.

The editors of *Sequence* were in youthful, impatient reaction against the propagandist efforts of the documentaries of the thirties, the restrictions of film production during the war years, the current critical denigration of American cinema, and the unimaginative and stagnant world of the British studios, Anderson and his colleagues fought for restoration of a lost sense of poetry in the contemporary film. Anderson's early critical essays, therefore,reflect several interests: the importance of a point of view in a film, the centrality of the director, the value of freshness and spontaneity, and the necessity for a poetic vision. In article after article, Anderson discussed these issues. He praised low budget films which seemed to capture a vitality missed by the studios. He attacked commercial producers for their preoccupation with profits and safe but dull projects. He demanded that film critics make their prejudices known and take a stand for better films and more humane ones. He criticized Rossellini's *Paisa* for its lack of message. He took Roger Manvell to task for becoming a booster of British films rather than a critic of them. In essays such as "Creative Elements," he tried to explain how films were put together by the interaction of many complex elements.[2] By praising what he felt was good and by condemning what he knew was bogus, he sought to encourage better cinema.

In such articles as "Angles of Approach," Anderson called upon critics to judge films by their intention. "Perceive the object of a film," he wrote, and then "judge its success in achieving that object."[3] In sharpening his perception of films and by pursuing his critical task by informing his audience, Anderson learned how films were made. He wrote about the complexity of the imaginative cinematic experience in "Creative Elements" and he implored critics to isolate and evaluate the various elements in each film, thereby helping the viewer understand the film experience more clearly.[4] One of the primary targets for Anderson during these years was the British studio system. He felt that the studios, because of their preoccupation with profit and their bureaucratic structure, were stifling young filmmakers. In "A Possible Solution," Anderson suggested that an avant-garde movement of independent producers might provide the competition to rejuvenate the industry which had become all too protected from criticism. He took the industry to task in "British Cinema: The Descending Spiral." In this essay Anderson noted the imperceptible impact of the British documentary on feature films produced by the studios. This situation was remedied over the next few years by, among others, Anderson himself.[5]

Anderson seemed drawn to the problems faced by filmmakers, as his essays on Hitchcock and Ford demonstrate. In "The Director's Cinema?" Anderson explored the film world of John Ford. He affirmed the central role played by a unifying creative intelligence in the creation of successful films. In a long discussion of Ford's *They Were Expendable*, Anderson discussed Ford's true interest in the reality of the world rather than in the symbolism of literary invention. Anderson felt that Ford had a natural poetic ability and a mastery over the medium which allowed him to create films which could be enjoyed by anyone. He had retained his sensitivity and subscribed to values which were primarily humane. Anderson has in his own films tried very hard to follow Ford's example.[6]

Anderson's reviews for *Sequence* and, after 1950, for *Sight and Sound*, therefore, reflect his wide experience with films and film styles. The yearly reports he filed from the Cannes Film Festival demonstrate his exposure to a broad spectrum of new and interesting films. His involvement in editing his book, *Making a Film: The Story of "Secret People,"*[7] allowed him to observe the process of creating a feature-length film at a time when he was first beginning his own filmmaking career in documentaries. His background in documentary film generated such pieces as "Only Connect: Some Aspects of Humphrey Jennings" in which he praised Jennings for being the only real poet Britain had yet produced in film. Jennings' poetic qualities surfaced in his handling of the everyday people in his war documentaries. It is something of this same poetic quality which distinguishes Anderson's *Thursday's Children* and *Every Day Except Christmas.*[8]

By the time he came to write "Notes from Sherwood," Anderson had established his critical and aesthetic criteria for judging films. He was familiar with the best of the Hollywood studios as well as the newest avant-garde continental films. In his essay "Stand Up! Stand Up!" he voiced his belief in the need for committed criticism.[9] The critic, and one must also assume the filmmaker, should not be impersonal in his reaction to cinema. He should hold firm political and social beliefs and not be afraid to state them openly. This essay marks the beginning of a much stronger emphasis on political involvement and commitment which Anderson advocated over the next few years. The ideas in this essay are also themes which surfaced in his films. The Free Cinema manifestos and "Get Out and Push!" reinforced Anderson's position on involvement. In these and similar articles and reviews he called for a revolution in the British movie industry. By 1958 and the publication of these views, however, Anderson was moving into the theater world which he would inhabit for the next five years without making a film. The same year also signaled Anderson's gradual withdrawal from film criticism. *Sequence* had folded six years before and he had gradually stopped writing for *Sight and Sound.* Now Anderson moved into an entirely new field of creative endeavor.

During most of the period when Anderson was writing film criticism, he was also learning how to make films. From his first documentary in 1948 until *Every Day Except Christmas* made in 1958, Anderson pursued a dual vocation. During those years he was learning the craft of cinema, and he provided himself with the underpinnings of a career as a filmmaker. His experience as a critic aided him in defining the role of the director and the need for a poetic vision. Just as the film critic of the cinema must hold and display his personal and political beliefs, so too the creator in films must have a credo which is apparent in his creations. As anyone who is familiar with the films of Lindsay Anderson knows, he carried over into his films the same commitment to critical and political values that he maintained as a film reviewer.

II

Lindsay Anderson shot his first film in 1958 for Richard Sutcliffe Ltd., a conveyor belt manufacturing company based in the Midlands. The film, *Meet the Pioneers*, is a straightforward industrial movie about the manufacture and installation of conveyors. Before making this film Anderson had no experience behind the camera, and he had only two years of background as a film reviewer and critic for *Sequence*. Even in this movie, however, there are scenes characteristic of Anderson's later work, for right in the middle of the film he caught the factory workers during their lunch break in images reminiscent of the best war documentaries of Humphrey Jennings. It is Anderson's attention to detail and the loving way he photographs each face and the musical rhythms of the editing as he carefully builds our understanding of these workers by their attitudes while at rest from their jobs, which makes this sequence a characteristic one. This keen observance of human beings in a natural setting highlights most of Anderson's documentary work and forms the absolute basis of *O Dreamland, Thursday's Children,* and *Every Day Except Christmas.*

With the exception of *The Wakefield Express*, the early industrial films are undistinguished but workmanlike projects. On them Anderson learned the business of making films. By the completion of *Three Installations* in 1952, he had discovered that editing was not just sticking bits of film together in accordance with some preconceived plan, and that sound tracks did not need to be narrated to the film but could be edited as well. By the time he came to *The Wakefield Express,* he had acquired Walter Lassally as his cameraman and John Fletcher as his production assistant. Their presence undoubtedly helped to give this movie a polish the others lacked. Anderson also had a wider range on this documentary so that the film became not just a study of the Wakefield newspaper, but a portrait of the whole community and, in miniature, the North of England. This project helped him to better understand that section of England which had been largely overlooked by the British cinema. His familiarity with the geography of the Midlands gave his first feature film, *This Sporting Life,* an authentic look.[10]

Cinematically 1953 marks a breakthrough for Anderson. In that year he made *Thursday's Children* with Guy Brenton and *O Dreamland.* For the first time he had projects which were totally of his own choosing, unrestrained by a sponsor. The film he did with Brenton was truly collaborative and it is difficult to determine how much of it was Anderson's. The contrast with *O Dreamland* is dramatic. Both documentaries are characterized by a careful attention to detail and a focus on people. *Thursday's Children,* however, is a gentle and loving study of the deaf children at the Margate School.[11] In spite of the fact that the film deals with children struggling against an enormous handicap, it is full of hope and warmth. *O Dreamland,* on the other hand, is harsh and biting. Anderson not only records the empty pleasures of the amusement park but satirizes and attacks them. Unlike Richard Burton's soothing narration for *Thursday's Children,* the sound track of *O Dreamland* is raucous and pinched like the pleasures it underscores. *Thursday's Children* and *O Dreamland* reflect a contrast which appears in Anderson's later films. He gets his message across by utilizing a combination of compassion and satire, and there are elements of both approaches in all of his films.

O Dreamland, instead of being the private film he had intended it to be, suddenly became a cause célèbre by appearing on the first of the Free Cinema programs. The Free Cinema Committee issued a manifesto which defined what a film should contain:

No film can be too personal.
The image speaks. Sound amplifies and comments.
Size is irrelevant. Perfection is not an aim.
An attitude means a style. A Style means an attitude.
Implicit in our attitude is a belief in freedom, in the importance of people and in the significance of the everyday.[12]

O Dreamland, not surprisingly, is everything a Free Cinema film should be. Certainly it is personal and had a style. The sound track both amplifies and comments on the images. These people should have more than this to choose from, Anderson seems to be saying; they are human beings and should not be degraded in this way. The on-location shooting necessitated some sacrifices in quality, but the film is not amateur and it does have a crude vitality. The lack of slickness is in itself refreshing.[13]

With this film Anderson made a statement. He not only put into practice those tenets of cinema which he had been preaching about in print for so long, but he also established a standard of filmmaking for himself. In *O Dreamland* he discovered the themes which he would pursue through his evolving style up to the present. *O Dreamland* also established the difference between those projects which Anderson would follow because he found them personally engaging, and those he would pursue in order to make money. The former would carry the burden of his personal vision; the latter would finance the films.

Over the next four years Anderson shot a number of short commissioned films for the National Society for the Prevention of Cruelty to Children (NSPCC), the National Industrial Fuel Efficiency Service, and the Central Office of Information for the Ministry of Agriculture, Fisheries, and Food. All of these shorts were made through Basic Films. Even in these commercials, one can see some early versions of themes which were later worked out in greater detail. Certainly the city/country contrast which appears in *Green and Pleasant Land,* one of the NSPCC films, was echoed in *O Lucky Man!,* even to the associations with Blake which both films have. The boys' chorus on the sound track of that same film, which is used in a contrasting way with the images, was used again in *If . . .* with much the same effect. A number of such specific techniques emerged in these short films.

By 1957, with *Every Day Except Christmas,* Anderson had reached the end of his apprenticeship. Even though this film was sponsored by the Ford Motor Company of Britain, Anderson was given a free hand with his subject matter and his approach. The result is a film assured in style and personal in content. But with the exception of *The Singing Lesson,* it was the last documentary Anderson was to make. In it he brought together many of those themes which infused his earlier films. It is a very humane film, one which takes as its subject matter the British working man and treats him not in a sociological way but in a vibrant and poetic way. Throughout his film criticism Anderson called for poetic films. In *Every Day Except Christmas,* he created one of his own. In a quiet way the film follows simple people as they perform their daily tasks, and Anderson captures the joy and good humor of the Covent Garden workers. Because the market attracts goods from all over the island, it is a microcosm for the British Isles. The narration stresses this connection as does the use of "God Save the Queen" when played over the radio at close-down as the trucks drive to London through the middle of the night. This is not the last time Anderson used one small section of English society as a metaphor for the whole. We see here in the labor of these men and women the dignity and good humor of the English people. The simple humanity of the workers mirrors the best that is in the English character. As Humphrey Jennings, in his documentaries, had captured the courage and pride of these same people during the war, so too Anderson sees identical traits in peace time. He does so with a simple straightforward style. It is not a didactic film. It is a film with a point of view, but one presented with the careful and skillful use of images tied together by Anderson's expressive editing and perceptive camera. It is a comfortable fusing of content and style which creates a poetic film[14]

In spite of its relative success, however, *Every Day Except Christmas* was Anderson's last film for the next six years. During that period he was unable to obtain studio backing for his cinema projects. In the meantime he worked in the theater, and in the process increased his ability to work with actors. It is obvious from his later films, especially his four major ones, that he learned his lessons well. Without exception these films reflect his talent as a director who obtains the best from the actors. Richard Harris turned in a *tour de force* performance in *This Sporting Life* and the handling of the ensemble in both *If...* and *O Lucky Man!* demonstrated Anderson's ability to individualize even the most minor characters. The acting of *In Celebration* is extraordinary.[15]

III

Anderson's first major film grew out of his interest in David Storey's novel *This Sporting Life* which he discovered in 1960. His lack of rapport with the studios, however, seemed to eliminate the possibility of his making the film version of the novel. It was not until several years later when Karel

Reisz turned down the chance to film the book that Anderson got his opportunity to direct a feature length film.

The movie posed a challenge. Anderson wanted to capture the intensely personal nature of the book which relies heavily on first person narration and flashbacks. Although a few of the critics of the film have complained about what they felt was a clumsy handling of the flashback material, one of the major achievements of the picture is the skillful manipulation of time.[16] Anderson does not lose the attention of the audience even though he dispenses with the traditional Hollywood devices for alerting the viewer to changes in time. Anderson never plays down to his audience but rather relies on his skill as a filmmaker to coerce his audience into becoming co-creators.[17] At times he may overestimate the visual sophistication of that audience, but apparently he finds that preferable to pandering to the lowest common denominator. The technique in *This Sporting Life*, unlike that in the films of Jean-Luc Godard with whom Anderson has occasionally been compared, is not obtrusive. The play of time in the film, the alternating between the past and the present, is skillfully done. The movie fits together well, and although there are a couple of awkward scenes, most notably the one in the restaurant with Machin and Mrs. Hammond, and the death bed scene at the hospital near the end of the film, the film evidences an unusual coherence.

Although the style of the film has been compared with the *nouvelle vague* and perhaps reflects Anderson's knowledge of French cinema, the subject matter is very British and echoes a number of themes which Anderson had explored in his earlier films. First, of course, is the north of England working-class background of the film. Anderson was familiar with the region of Storey's novel because of his work on the Sutcliffe films. In fact, he discovered later that while making those films in Yorkshire he was actually shooting just a few miles from where Storey himself was growing up. *This Sporting Life*, however, can in no way be called a working-class film in the manner of Karel Reisz's *Saturday Night and Sunday Morning* or Tony Richardson's *The Loneliness of the Long Distance Runner*. The story was set in the north of England but the region was not the focus of the film. Frank Machin is working-class, but the film does not center on him as a representative of his class. Even though *This Sporting Life* is mildly leftist in its portrayal of the exploitation of Machin by the capitalist class, it is not Marxist in tone.[18] All of these considerations are secondary to the main theme which is the relationship between his principal characters, Machin and Mrs. Hammond. Even the rugby scenes which are so effectively photographed, especially the slow motion sequence which concludes the film, are subordinated to the frustrated passion of what one critic unfortunately called the footballer and the lady.[19]

By his innovative use of the flashback, Anderson manages to avoid the look and atmosphere of the "kitchen sink" films which by 1963 had become almost a convention in British cinema. Without copying his fellow directors, he remained true to the propositions he had helped them articulate in the Free Cinema manifestos, namely, that British films should concern themselves with emotions, the working class, the England outside of the home counties, and social and political issues. Anderson touches on all of these in *This Sporting Life*, but does so in a very human context and not at all in a programmatic manner. He does not allow the issues to dominate the film; his people do. Although Anderson has always been considered a political director, a reputation which became especially pronounced with the upheaval created by *If . . .* and the timeliness of that film, he has never made a motion picture primarily dedicated to advocating a particular system or political philosophy. His vision encompasses the world in all of its complexity and diversity. He has assiduously avoided a doctrinaire position which would reduce the multiplicity of the human experience to a simple and thereby simple-minded thesis. In *Every Day Except Christmas, Thursday's Children,* and *O Dreamland,* Anderson trained his camera on the human face, and in the manner of Humphrey Jennings created a composite of the British people. In *This Sporting Life* he focused on Frank Machin, not as a representative of a class, but as an individual who possessed all of the contraditions and complexity that being human entails.

Among the strengths which emerged from the making of *This Sporting Life* was the obvious skill with which Anderson employs actors. The performances of both the principals, Rachael Roberts and Richard Harris, are extremely strong. Both of them, in fact, won considerable recognition for the roles they portrayed.[20] It is not just with the principal characters, however, that Anderson excels. One of the distinctive features of all of his major films has been the skillful employment of his supporting ensemble. Anderson has given his secondary players the attention rarely seen in films today. Their performances are extremely good, so good in fact that often one remains unaware until later of the fine work of the major figures. He has used Arthur Lowe in a wide variety of roles in four of his films; Mona Washbourne has appeared with frequency as does Peter Jeffery and Bill Owen; and Rachael Roberts, who had a leading role in *This Sporting Life,* played supporting roles in *O Lucky Man!* One of the exciting experiences of Anderson's cinema is to see how he will use familiar characters in new and demanding settings.

This use of the same actors in film after film is not just based on friendship or convenience, although both elements may be factors; instead, it is indicative of Anderson's whole approach to cinema. He is constantly experimenting within a tradition. Just as he has repeatedly used the same techniques with increasing sophistication, such as the episodic presentation of material which began in *The White Bus,* he has also reiterated themes. Many of the primary concerns which dominated the early documentaries, such as the workaday world in the Sutcliffe films and *Every Day Except Christmas,* appear in minor ways in later feature films, sometimes lovingly treated, often satirized. The observation of the crowds at the Dreamland amusement park which made that film so effective appears later in *The Singing Lesson* with much the same effect. The multiple use of the same actors fits into this same interest in continuity; they are known quantities which sometimes provide linkages with previous films.[21]

At the same time that Anderson is reworking old themes and techniques he is also changing and innovating within the familiarity of his tradition. For example, he did use music in *O Dreamland* for commentary as the Free Cinema group had suggested. But in *O Lucky Man!* the music was not only used to comment on the visual action, but in fact became one of the major structural devices of the film. The episodic nature of *The White Bus* gave way to the more sharply divided scenes in *The Singing Lesson,* which in turn evolved into the formal divisions of *If . . .* and *O Lucky Man!.* From the beginning of his career as a film professional, whether as a critic or filmmaker, Anderson has interested himself in the extension of the expressive possibilities of the medium.

In the years between *This Sporting Life* and *If . . .,* Anderson once again devoted his energies primarily to the theater. There were two exceptions however. He began to make television commercials and he directed two short films, *The White Bus* and *The Singing Lesson.* He made the commercials for the money. Anderson has always felt that it is far easier to make advertisements than to shoot long commercial films when he needs an income. The commercials are short, easy to make, and require no outlay of emotional energy. Even the creative energy they require is minimal. They have kept him within the world of the commercial film, and from this work he has obviously gained experience in compressing information into short episodes.

This structural technique which has become almost a trademark of Anderson's films was first used extensively in the medium-length film *The White Bus* which he made as a part of a trilogy produced by Woodfall Films. In *The White Bus* Anderson develops his story in a series of vignettes in which the central character, a girl from the north of England who is working in London as a secretary, returns home to discover that she does not fit into that environment any more. From the beginning Anderson demonstrated that the film would not be straightforward exposition. As with Machin, who slips in and out of the present in *This Sporting Life,* the girl here projects her fantasies onto the world around her. The film, however, does not even employ the flashback technique of the previous film. Anderson allows his character to move back and forth between fantasy and reality without resorting to film convention. The bizarre actions of the characters in *The White Bus* alert the audience to the changing perceptions of the heroine, as does the shifting between color and black and white photography.

Once again the film deals with an individual against society. This time the girl is more conscious of what her perceptions of that society are. Machin feels things, the wrongs, and the frustrations, but is unable to verbalize those feelings or to understand what is happening to him. He does not know how to react against the world except with brute strength. The girl is far more perceptive, and we are given more of her point of view. This movement inward prepared the way for the subjectivity of *If...*, and made clear that the adolescents in that film slide in and out of a fantasy world that is as real for them as the actual world. It is an interesting technique and immensely disturbing since the audience is constantly kept off balance.

If *The White Bus* looks forward to Anderson's more subjective and complex films of the late sixties and early seventies, *The Singing Lesson* in its simplicity and freshness harkens back to Anderson's earlier documentaries. It is a charming film, full of the enthusiasm of the students and their instructor at the Warsaw Dramatic Academy. Anderson divided the project into six sections, each one containing a song. He intercut these song sequences with footage shot of the people of Warsaw. The contrasts are striking, especially of the tired crowds returning home at the end of the film. Anderson captures the people of the city with the same astuteness he used in *Every Day Except Christmas* or *O Dreamland*. One sees the students creating something poetic out of the prosaic life around them. This theme of the artist or performer as shaper and maker of reality has obviously fascinated Anderson for some time. It is an every present element in his films, but does not actually surface until the end of *O Lucky Man!* when Anderson, as himself, makes his gesture as creator by slapping Malcolm McDowell with a rolled up script.[22] That notion, however, of the shaping nature of art and the contrasts between art and reality are implicit in *The Singing Lesson*. It is not a schematic film, though, and one comes away from it not with a weighty sense of having been instructed but rather with the delight of having been entertained. If anything is disquieting about the experience it is seeing the exuberance and hopes of the young actors juxtaposed with the dreary and often tedious world outside the studio. With added menace this is the same theme Anderson pursued at greater length in *O Lucky Man!*

It is a shame that neither *The White Bus* nor *The Singing Lesson* have been widely shown, since they provide the artistic links between *This Sporting Life* and *If...*,[23] For those critics who were confused by *If...*, these two intermediate films have much to reveal. The techniques as well as subject matter are extensions of Anderson's previous career. His increasing competence with the camera as well as his growing ability to handle an ensemble of actors were not just the results of his commercial television work and theater directing.

Although *The White Bus* and *The Singing Lesson* were commercially unviable and critically ignored, Anderson's next film was successful in both respects, so successful in fact that it brought him wide popular recognition as a director and made him, for a while at least, something of a guru to the student generation of the sixties. *If...*, rather unexpectedly, came at precisely the right moment to capture the spirit of youthful rebellion in the United States. It was prophetic. The same issue of the *New York Times* which carried notices of the film also carried photographs of students at Cornell University brandishing guns and upraised closed fists.[24] Anderson could not have foreseen the violent events of the late sixties when he began to work on the film, but obviously he did perceive a need to treat rebellious youth, and did so in a way which displays a deep understanding of the nature of adolescent rejection of authority and fantasy. Much of the film is also autobiographical in that it suggests something of Anderson's own rebellious temperment. The youthful rebels of the world of *If...* actualized their fantasies. Instead of idle dreaming or isolated self-destructive violence, the students pushed their fantasies onto the world they want to change. For Anderson, who was interested in pursuing the complexities between dream and reality, it is not difficult to discover in the current of rebellion a frightening possibility. In a world of violence and changing social and moral structures would it not be possible for youthful revolutionaries to carry out their dreams? Anderson seems to be implying that if society continues to train its youth to be violent, as soldiers for example, then perhaps society must be ready to accept violent acts which escape the narrow context for which they were intended.

In *If...* Anderson proposes that the microcosm of the school could stand for society as a whole and need not be confined to just the world of adolescent boys. The same social and political pressures for yielding to the system exist within the school environment that exist outside in a broader social context. Unlike Vigo's *Zero for Conduct,* to which *If...* has often been compared and to which Anderson himself has acknowledged his debt, the rebelliousness of Anderson's adolescents is far more sinister than the youthful pranks of Vigo's French schoolboys of a generation before. The thoughts of Mick and his compatriots are violent and hateful and much closer to the world inhabited by the youth of *The Loneliness of the Long Distance Runner* or the milieu of Antoine Doinel in Truffaut's *The 400 Blows*. Like Machin in *This Sporting Life* and the girl in *The White Bus*, these rebels are outsiders, but in this case outsiders who do not want to get in. It is tempting to extend the discussion of the characters in *If...* to include *O Lucky Man!*, and indeed Anderson invites us to do so since he gives the same name to the character played by the same actor in both films and there are several allusions to *If...* in the later film. One is left at the end of *If...* with the extended shot Anderson holds of Mick glaring into the camera. The image is one of intransigence. He obviously hates what all those people stand for; he obviously wants to destroy them. It may be that Anderson ultimately saw the rebellion failing, leaving the youth of the sixties to fend for themselves. Perhaps they did go out into the world with a wide-eyed innocence and tried to fit in. Perhaps they sold out and tried to "make it" in the most traditional sense. These reflections, however, are antecedent to the final message of *If....*[25]

What is most exciting about *If...* is not the subject matter of the film, but the film itself. It is beautifully photographed. Miroslav Ondricek supported Anderson's conception as did the production design of Jocelyn Herbert. The warm tones of the buildings which suggest the traditions of private school contrast sharply with the cruelty and barbarism within. Mick's collection of posters and photographs, some of female nudes and others of black revolutionaries, provides a revealing antithesis to his formal school attire with its Eton collar and tie. The repeated visits to the chapel which frame the acts of rebellion on the part of Mick and his friends heighten this contrast between what the college appears to be and what it is. The most evocative stylistic device which Anderson uses is the unexpected passing in and out of the boys' fantasy world.

With very little warning Anderson begins about midway through the film to include passages which are a part of the escapist world of the boys' dreams. By the end of the film we as an audience are experiencing the world almost totally from the boys' perspective. The obvious point is that the boys themselves often do not distinguish between fantasy and reality, or reality has become so fantastic that the distinctions are specious. In order for the viewer to understand the world of these young men, he too must have trouble discriminating between the two.

Some of the critics have been less than complimentary about his use of this artifice, claiming that one gets lost in the film because of it.[26] These complaints sound very much like the arguments used against the flashback segments of *This Sporting Life*. On the contrary, the approach works extremely well. We are drawn into the film with an intensity which would be missing if Anderson had used a more conventional approach to the fantasy sequences. The world of *If...* at least appears normal, ordered, and traditional. The message which Anderson is putting across and forcing upon his viewers with the fierce denouement is that the possible consequences of retaining a traditional moral code in the face of a rapidly changing world must be seen. It is no longer viable to force outdated traditions upon youth, especially if those traditions were designed to produce citizens for a far different world.

Many of the hostile critics were bothered by what they felt was the uncertainty of style and the disastrous finish. Stanley Kauffmann was particularly outspoken about what he felt was the "unsyntactical and ruinous" ending to *If....* He has been equally critical of the conclusions of *This Sporting Life* and *O Lucky Man!*, and his concerns have bothered other critics as well.[27] Many of the reviewers have noted Anderson's talent while deploring the unevenness of his style. Richard Schickel complained that, according to all the film theories he knew, *If . . .* should not work at all. On the other hand, David Spiers writing for *Screen* suggested that Anderson's style was spare and provided his audience with the essentials of the film in an unobtrusive way. What to do with Anderson's presentation of his materials is one of the unanswered critical questions about his film.[28]

In between completing *If . . .* and beginning *O Lucky Man!,* Anderson went back to shooting commercials and directing plays, and publicizing his film. In fact it was on one of the publicity tours for *If . . .* that Malcolm McDowell and David Sherwin, script writer for *If . . .,* began their collaboration on *O Lucky Man!* The gestation for the new film really began before the experience of the previous one had ended. With his new film Anderson was able to draw on many of the same talents he had used before: McDowell, Sherwin, Ondricek, and Medwin. Anderson was assembling a stock company much in the same way that John Ford, one of the directors Anderson had most admired, put together a like-minded group of film people in his later days in Hollywood.

Anderson makes clear that *O Lucky Man!* takes off from where *If . . .* left off. The central character is once again mischieveously perhaps misleadingly called Mick, a Mick greatly changed from *If . . .,* but Mick nonetheless. Anderson creates in him a modern-day Candide, an innocent who is battered by the corruption of the world. He is another of Anderson's outsiders who, like Machin, is desperately trying to get in. Mick wants to make it. By following the traditional value structures of society he hopes to gain prosperity and social position. He perseveres through the film as he is shunted in different directions by each authority figure he meets. It is in some ways the reverse of *If . . .,* in which Mick rebels against everything and everyone who is in authority. In *O Lucky Man!* he conforms almost completely. His treatment out in the world is horrifying. He is swindled, beaten by government agents, imprisoned because he is betrayed by his employer, seduced by practically every woman he meets, and finally almost killed by the "down and outs" he is trying to help. He is ultimately rescued by Anderson himself who appears in the movie as a film director casting for a movie—*If . . . .* When Anderson hits him on the face with a rolled up script, Mick experiences a moment of illumination, perceives the world as it is, and realizes how he is to survive it.[29] This echoes the discussion earlier in the film when Mick listens to the talk about Zen on the radio. Anderson does not spell all of this out but merely hints at it by having Mick deliver a rather enigmatic smile into the camera. It is quite a contrast from the ferocity of the defiant shot at the conclusion of *If . . . .*[30]

Obviously we, as the audience, are the ones who are receiving through the medium of the motion picture, a shock of recognition as well. We, along with Mick, have reached a moment of insight. Anderson has taken us along on Mick's odyssey for good reason. He want us to recognize what Mick is able to recognize, namely that the world is a place of moral and physical corruption, and that we must learn to understand it—and perhaps so to transcend it. It seems to be the only conclusion one can draw from Mick's experience. One must have some luck and learn how to accept life without being destroyed. Anderson has written that acceptance is not conformism. The filmmaker is one who, through the manipulation of his medium, can provide his viewers with insight into the world around them. Anderson has never abandoned the task of educating people which he first learned while shooting his documentaries. *O Lucky Man!* is a fable with the traditional moral.[31]

Anderson's films have become progressively more political in nature. Unlike Costa-Gavras, however, Anderson's films are not overtly political which is one of the reasons why "liberal" movie reviewers often find him difficult to understand. He has moved from his concentration on one man's frustration and failure to a broader concern with society as a whole. His view is a rather grim one. Social structures seem to abstruct personal development and impede the growth of individual talent. Perhaps there is a bit of Anderson's own experience reflected in the message of these films. He too has been a rebel and received some rather severe disappointments in his career. Like most artists, he has not been adequately rewarded for either his insight into the nature of man or for his perceptions about the function of social and political institutions. He has exposed too much hypocrisy and fraud to be widely praised. One should expect this intransigence from him. A cursory glance at the criticism he wrote for *Sequence* or for *Sight and Sound* will demonstrate how tough and uncompromising he has always been. Even his earlier films, especially *O Dreamland,* have demonstrated his keen insight into human experience. *O Lucky Man!* is no exception; it made a lot of people uncomfortable.

The last film Anderson made was an anomolous one since it is a filmed play. In 1974 Anderson shot a film version of David Storey's play "In Celebration" for the American Film Theater. Anderson had directed the London production and used the original cast in the film. It is an extraordinary experience. More than the film of a play, that bastard genre which seems to satisfy no one, it is a play which has been successfully translated into the medium of film. *In Celebration* does not fit very neatly into the flow of his other films, however, which makes it a problem to analyze in that context. In and of itself it is a first-rate piece of film, but the restrictions placed upon Anderson by the script and the need to retain the qualities of the original drama for the American Film Theater series somewhat hampered his execution. At least one critic has always felt that Anderson worked best when he was restrained by a tight script drawn from a source other than his own imagination. This film is certainly tightly structured. It is restrained and crisply done. The camera moves outside the one set of the play only occasionally and does so smoothly and without calling attention to itself. These interludes are not intrusions or added scenes obviously shot for the film, but rather organic parts of the drama itself.[32]

The acting is superb. It is sheer joy to watch the performances in the production. In part the success of the venture was due to Anderson's comfort with both media. He knows how to handle actors and space on the stage, and he can manipulate with equal skill the world of the screen. If this film resembles any of his previous ones it would have to be *This Sporting Life*. Both stories deal with intense emotional situations. The focus is on that tension as well as in the alienation of the working-class boys from their background. In fact, the world of *In Celebration* is almost claustrophobic, and such concentration is one of the reasons for the play's impact. We as an audience are trapped in this confining space, and forced to watch the disclosure of the family's secrets, even though perhaps we would like to avoid the confrontation. The film insists on our attention, and we are drained by the experience.

One of the goals Anderson set out to accomplish with his films was to root out the middle-class stodginess of British cinema, and to introduce some passion into a tradition of placid films. With *In Celebration* he goes a long way in furthering that goal. Unlike the restrained characters of *If . . .* and *O Lucky Man!* who, when they respond to their world at all, do so with a lack of passion, the characters in *In Celebration* explode on the screen like Machin and Mrs. Hammond before them.

IV

Among the tenets of the Free Cinema group was an insistence that British cinema move beyond the confines of the home counties which surround London. Certainly Anderson has helped to make that happen. He has explored in some depth the industrial midlands in his documentaries and in three of his four feature films. The location has provided more than a background for the films; it has been a positive force in shaping them. As a corollary to filming the North he has examined the people of that region as well.

One of the areas which bothered Anderson the most when he was writing criticism of other people's films was their lack of commitment, their lack of dedication. Too many middle-class British films carefully avoided anything that smacked of politics or social criticism. The film directors seemed afraid to take on an attitude which would involve them in the political arena. Anderson despised this cowardice, and his films have consistently projected a social and political awareness. Practically everything he has done contains implied if not overt criticism of conventional social attitudes, and although his political leanings have been associated with the left, he has not become doctrinaire or in any way blinded by ideology; he is perfectly capable of distinguishing the bogus from the true no matter what the political alliance. In the film *If...*, Anderson suggests that there is a great deal worth preserving in the system of the private school, even though that institution has been for years the target of those who would do away with the class system in England. For Anderson as well as many other traditional socialists in Great Britain, the modern welfare state has not necessarily provided the utopia which more naive leftists had expected. There is still much inhumanity, stupidity, arrogance, and exploitation which needs to be expelled before the world truly becomes the place of opportunity and security it should be.

Anderson's final vision is the world as a frightening place, and he sees all of us menaced at every turn by the government, science, big business, and the media. Even the traditional sources of succor like the church have failed. It is a world in which, like Mick, all must wander alone and often defenseless, to be preyed upon by every manner of horrors. It is a place where every haven harbors unimaginable terrors. Perhaps the only salvation is in the experience of the artist who gives others, in his creations, glimpses of the world which are true and clear and which will force confrontation with corruption and failure. Perhaps the artist's vision can convince others to become committed to action, to fight for what is decent and right, not only for themselves, but for everyone as well.

Anderson does not propose any program or diagram for repairing social malfunctions. He does however offer us a suggestion on how to begin. First look at the world with clarity; eliminate the bogus; cut through the hypocrisy; deny the inhumane, because then and only then can we truly discover our humanity and in the process, the humanity of others. His role as filmmaker is to attract our attention, to focus it in the right direction, to shock us, to anger us, and to do anything which will arouse us from the lethargy of contemporary life. Anderson is a man of passion, one who cares deeply, and he has used his considerable talent to invite us to share in his commitment.

NOTES

1. "Notes from Sherwood," *Sight and Sound*, 26, No. 3 (Winter 1956), 159-165.
2. Review of *Paisa* (Ordinary People), *Sequence*, 2 (Winter 1947), 30-31; "The Manvell Approach," *Sequence*, 2 (Winter 1947), 34-35; "Creative Elements," *Sequence*, 5 (Autumn 1948), 8-12.
3. "Angles of Approach," *Sequence*, 2 (Winter 1947), 71-72. This is the first of several essays in which Anderson tried to formulate his critical beliefs.
4. See #2 above for "Creative Elements."
5. "A Possible Solution," *Sequence*, 3 (Spring 1948), 7-10 and "British Cinema: The Descending Spiral," *Sequence* 7 (Spring 1949), 6-11. Anderson felt that since the war critics had been too easy on the British film industry. This attitude had

taken on economic and political overtones because the industry's survival depended upon continued support from within the British Isles. Anderson was sympathetic with the plight of the industry but thought that such privilege was not helping what he felt was the vacuity of English films.

6. "Films of Alfred Hitchcock," *Sequence,* 9 (Autumn 1949), 113-124; "The Director's Cinema?" *Sequence,* 12 (Autumn 1950), 6-11, 37; "They Were Expendable and John Ford," *Sequence,* 11 (Summer 1950), 18-31. Anderson reviewed a number of Ford pictures over the years, and although his estimation of Ford's abilities as a director never changed, Anderson was disappointed with some of his later films. He wrote more about Ford than any other director.

7. *Making a Film: The Story of "Secret People."* (London: Allen and Unwin, 1952). This book contains a daily account of the filming of Thorold Dickinson's *Secret People.* The experience obviously was a valuable one for Anderson for he had the opportunity to trace the development of a film from its very inception to the final print.

8. "Only Connect: Some Aspects of the Work of Humphrey Jennings," *Sight and Sound,* 23, No. 4 (April-June 1953), 181-183, 186. Anderson felt a particular affection for the work of Jennings. He believed that the war brought out the best in his films because it fired his passions in a way no other event had been able to do. One speculates whether it hasn't been a similar kindling of passions which politics has created in Anderson and thereby galvanized him into making the best of his films.

9. "Stand Up! Stand Up!" *Sight and Sound,* 26, No. 2 (Autumn 1956), 63-93.

10. Elizabeth Sussex in her study of Anderson devotes a chapter to his early films and much of the factual information in this section was drawn from the interviews with Anderson which she capsulized for that chapter. *See* Elizabeth Sussex, "Early Films" in *Lindsay Anderson* (New York: Frederick A. Praeger, 1969), pp. 15-29.

11. *Thursday's Children* was awarded an Oscar as the best short subject of 1954 and was shown at least minimally on the cinema circuits. The excitement created by the Free Cinema showings stimulated interest in Anderson's documentaries in general and probably did more to promote *Thursday's Children* than the academy award did.

12. This statement was drawn from a four-page mimeographed handout supplied to me by the British Film Institute. The brochure spells out a little more fully the tenets listed here.

13. The importance of the Free Cinema movement cannot be overstated. It provided a forum for a number of dissident voices in British cinema during the mid-fifties. It was also unquestionably responsible, at least in part, for creating a climate which produced the renaissance of British films directed by Richardson, Anderson, Reisz, and Clayton, among others. It was a concrete and rather successful political attack on the stodgy British studio system which the *Sequence* editors had been sniping at for years.

14. In addition to the film experience he was acquiring from making his own films, Anderson was also engaged in other cinema related activities. He filmed five episodes of the Robin Hood television series during the 1955-56 season, was production manager for James Broughton's film *The Pleasure Garden,* was supervising editor on the *March to Aldermaston* for the eleven-member production committee, directed a film insert for Harry Cookson's play "The

Lily White Boys," and helped to edit two other films: *Together* by Lorenza Mazzetti and *Rekava* (*The Line of Life*) by Lester James Peries.

15. A number of reviewers have also found Anderson's stage training obtrusive. Peter Baker, for instance, thought that Anderson's long stint at the Royal Court was all too apparent from his film actor's lapses into stage performances. *See* Peter Baker, Review of *This Sporting Life, Films and Filming*, 9, No. 6 (March 1963), 32.

16. Perhaps the most virulent attack on Anderson's handling of time came in a hostile review of the film written by Jay Cocks. *See* Jay Cocks, "Slummox," *Time*, 82 (19 July 1963), 78.

17. Philip Hartung noted that Anderson's technique kept the audience on its toes by requiring it to work and think with the director. *See* Philip Hartung, *Commonweal*, 78 (August 1963), 480.

18. Tom Milne in an early review of the film noted that of all the Free Cinema directors Anderson was the one who had developed the "most recognizable, most personal style." Milne also was one of the first critics to notice that Anderson had not created just another north country film in the mode of *Room at the Top* but rather an individual study of the tragedy of Frank Machin. *See* Tom Milne, "This Sporting Life," *Sight and Sound*, 31, No. 3 (Summer 1962), 122.

19. Stanley Kauffmann has great difficulty dealing with Anderson's films. While he sees great talent in them, as a critic he also discovers great flaws in their conception. *See* Stanley Kauffmann, "The Footballer and the Lady," *New Republic*, 149 (20 June 1963), 25-26.

20. Richard Harris won the Grand Prize at Cannes in 1963 for his portrait of Machin, and both Harris and Rachael Roberts were nominated for academy awards.

21. Anderson struggles with the conventional ideas of tradition and discipline which form a large part of his background. By class, education, and heritage he should be much more bound by the classic British virtues than he is. There is an ambivalence in his films at times which suggests this conflict.

22. Anderson is often actually present in his own films, a practice which dates from his earliest documentaries. For example, *Trunk Conveyor* begins with Anderson shouting "O. K." on the sound track before rolling the credits.

23. *The White Bus* was exhibited briefly in London. As far as I can determine, *The Singing Lesson* has never been shown commercially, and only infrequently whenever Anderson retrospectives have been mounted. *See* John Coleman, "Big Tati," *New Statesman*, 76 (19 July 1968), 89-90; Gordon Gow, Review of *The White Bus, Films and Filming*, 14, No. 12 (September 1968), 42; and Daniel Millar, Review of *The White Bus, Sight and Sound*, 37, No. 4 (Autumn 1968), 205-206.

24. Russell Baker, in an editorial for *The New York Times*, defended *If . . .* against an onslaught of letter writers who were condemning the film for what they saw as its revolutionary message. *See* Russell Baker, "Observer: Youth Without Rose Colored Glasses," *The New York Times*, (13 May 1969), p. 46.

25. The critical response to *If . . .* was curious. A few of the reviewers pilloried Anderson for pandering to the youth with what they felt was a trendy film, and irresponsibly suggesting armed rebellion as a viable solution to contemporary problems. *See* Gary Arnold, "*If . . .*: Pop Rebellion, Fantasy, and Snob Appeal," *The Washington Post*, (13 June 1969), p. G3; Norman Cecil, Review of *If . . .*, *Films in Review*, 20, No. 4 (April 1969), 255-256; and most importantly, Pauline Kael, "School Days, School Days," *The New Yorker*, 45 (15 March 1969), 152, 154, 159-161.

26. The lack of traditional touchstones for the use of fantasy and the seemingly quixotic movement between color and black and white photography, which incidentally was quite accidental, were singled out as annoying aspects of the film. The critical consensus was, however, primarily favorable. Most of the critics praised Anderson's treatment of detail and the marvelous atmosphere of the film. *See* in particular: Robert Kotlowitz, "Aspects of Love," *Harpers,* 238 (April 1969), 115-116; Roger Ebert, "Student vs. the System in Bloody Vision, *Chicago Sun Times* (1 June 1969), section II, pp. 5, 8; and Gordon Gow, Review of *If...*, *Films and Filming,* 15, No. 6 (March 1969), 50-51.

27. I have singled out Kauffmann because he seems to summarize the questions which the more thoughtful critics have asked of Anderson's work. *See* Stanley Kauffmann, Review of *If...*, *New Republic,* 160 (15 February 1969), 22, and Review of *O Lucky Man!*, *New Republic,* 168 (16 June 1973), 24, 33.

28. Richard Schickel, "Angry Knot in the Old School Tie," *Life,* 66 (February 1969), 8, and David Spiers, Review of *If...*, *Screen,* 10, No. 2 (March-April 1969), 85-89.

29. One article in the *London Times* was even titled "*If...* Trio Turns to Candide." The piece mentions that Anderson would not discuss his new film except to say that it was concerned with what happens after one leaves school. *See* "The Times Diary: *If...* Trio Turn to Candide," the *Times* (London), (11 May 1971), p. 13.

30. John Coleman, "Zen He Go Walkabout," *New Statesman,* 85 (4 May 1973), 666. Contains a particularly biting attack on Anderson's hidden meaning within the film.

31. Some of the critics have been hard on *O Lucky Man!* They have complained of the film's length, of its diffuseness which was saved only by the use of Alan Price's music, and of the fuzziness of its meaning. *See* especially the following reviews: Loraine Alterman, "Yes, Rock Can Sometimes Save a Bad Movie," *The New York Times* (8 July 1973), section II, pp. 8, 19; Gary Arnold, "A Satirical Tale of Getting Ahead," *The Washington Post,* (20 June 1973), p. 11B; Vincent Canby, "O Lucky Man! Ran Out of Luck," *The New York Times,* (24 June 1973), section II, pp. 1, 13; W.S. Pechter, "Politics on Film," *Commentary,* 56 (September 1973), 74-77; and B. Rothenbuecher, "Not Yet a Man," *Christian Century,* 90 (15-22 August 1973), 809-810

32. The critics have been almost uniformly praiseworthy about this film, and they seem to like just about everything Anderson did with the play. *See* especially: Vincent Canby, "Storey's 'In Celebration' Is Moving Film," *The New York Times,* (18 March 1975), p. 30; Jay Cocks, "Dead Center," *Time,* 105 (17 February 1975), 4; Judith Crist, Review of *In Celebration, New York Magazine,* 8 (17 March 1975), 77; Molly Haskell, "The Truth Game," *Village Voice,* 20 (31 March 1975), 76-77; and Tads (J. P. Tadros), Review of *In Celebration, Variety,* 277 (22 January 1975), 35.

The Films: Synopses, Credits, and Notes

*1. MEET THE PIONEERS (1948)[1]

Producers:	Desmond and Lois Sutcliffe (Richard Sutcliffe Ltd.)
Director:	Lindsay Anderson
Photography:	John Jones,Edward Brendon
Editors:	Lindsay Anderson, Edward Brendon
Art Advisor:	Eric Westbrook
Music:	Len Scott
Commentator:	Lindsay Anderson
Running time:	33 minutes

Synopsis

Meet the Pioneers is a film about the conveyor belt manufacturing firm of Richard Sutcliffe Ltd. in Wakefield, England. The film shows how conveyor belts are used in coal mines "for the making of gas, for speeding up the packing of rug wool, for carrying limestone from a quarry in North Wales to await collection by the boats at sea." The film also describes the history of the factory and how the belts are made. There is a lengthy sequence showing the Sutcliffe workers at lunch. With the machines quiet we see people wandering out of doors and relaxing in various parts of the factory, workers chatting and reading newspapers, and people eating sandwiches. This scene is followed by a shot of the yards where the raw materials for the belts are kept. Then we are taken back into the factory for the afternoon shift.

Notes:

Anderson shot this film with a camera built to Air Force specifications which was purchased for £100 in Wardour Street. He used the local schoolmaster as his cameraman and Edward Brendon, who had been working as an assistant for British National, as his general assistant. Anderson narrated the film.

*2. IDLERS THAT WORK (1949)

Producer:	Richard O'Brian (Richard Sutcliffe Ltd.)
Director:	Lindsay Anderson
Photography:	George Levy
Music:	Ralph Vaughan Williams, Aaron Copland
Continuity:	Lois Sugcliffe
Unit Assistants:	Bill Longley, Geoff Oakes, Ernest Slinger, George Wilby
Commentator:	Lindsay Anderson
Running time:	17 minutes

Synopsis

This film, the second in the Sutcliffe series, deals with a particular component of the conveyors, the idlers. The idlers are the rollers underneath the conveyor belts. It is strictly an informational film on the function and manufacture of these parts.

Notes:

Anderson began another film after *Meet the Pioneers* which had to be scrapped because the camera jammed so often, so this film is actually the third Sutcliffe film that Anderson began. With a better camera (the original was scrapped after the aborted second film), and a more professional cameraman, George Levy, a camera assistant at Ealing Studios, the film has a more professional quality. Anderson once again read the commentary.

*3. THREE INSTALLATIONS (1952)

Producer:	Dermod Sutcliffe (Richard Sutcliffe Ltd.)
Director:	Lindsay Anderson
Photography:	Walter Lassally
Additional Photography	John Jones
Assistant Cameraman:	Desmond Davis
Editor:	Derek York
Orchestral Music:	Copland, Gillis, Khachaturian
Conveyor Boogie:	Alan Clare (piano), Johnny Flanagan (drums)
Sound:	Charles Green
Production Manager:	John Exley
Unit Assistant:	Vincent Young
Commentator:	Lindsay Anderson
Running time:	28 minutes

Synopsis

This film concentrates on three installations: an iron ore works, a cement works, and a project for the disposal of waste soil and slag. The film contains numerous panning shots which capture the sweep of the huge conveyor installations. Anderson used the music of Copland, Gillis, and Khachaturian to set the rhythm of the movie. The closing sequence is a series of superimposed shots which dissolve from the faces of the workers at the design boards to the full scale slag-shifting operation outside.

Notes:

On this film Anderson first used Walter Lassally as his cameraman, an association which lasted through a succession of documentaries. Lassally was not only a friend of John Fletcher's, but also of Derek York, with whom he later formed an amateur unit called Screencraft.

*4. TRUNK CONVEYOR (1952)[2]

Producer:	Dermod Sutcliffe (Richard Sutcliffe Ltd, National Coal Board)
Director:	Lindsay Anderson
Photography:	John Reid
Camera Assistant:	Gerry Godfrey
Editor:	Bill Mergarry
Assistant Editor:	James Vans Collina
Songs:	Bert Lloyd
Music:	Alf Edwards (concertina) Fitzroy Coleman (guitar)
Production Manager:	Peter Woodward
Commentator:	Lindsay Anderson
Running time:	38 minutes

Synopsis

Trunk Conveyor is another instructional/informational film about conveyor belts used in the coal industry. Anderson verbally cues in the film, and we see two fitters who stop to light their cigarettes before going to work. The technical and instructional passages are alternated by means of song sequences using "Sixteen Tons" and the "collier song." "Sixteen Tons" is used at the beginning while the men work and the coal runs along the conveyor. The "collier song" is used to accompany a coal truck which drives through the landscape and to introduce the miners as they emerge from the pit. "Sixteen Tons" is again used at the end of the film when we see the coal running along the newly-constructed conveyor.

Notes:

This was Anderson's last film for the Sutcliffes and on it he used John Reid, a cameraman for the coal board, instead of Lassally, who was unavailable. The film was shot almost entirely in a West Yorkshire colliery and used the safety lights of the coal board.

*5. WAKEFIELD EXPRESS (1952)

Producer:	Michael Robinson (The Wakefield Express Series Ltd.)
Director:	Lindsay Anderson

Photography:	Walter Lassally
Songs:	Snapethorpe and Horbury Secondary Modern Schools
Band Music:	Horbury Victoria Prize Band
Production	
Assistant:	John Fletcher
Commentator:	George Potts
Running time:	33 minutes

Synopsis

The film opens on a shot of a typewriter with the sounds of typing and the laughter of children in the background. It cuts to a reporter, notebook in hand, interviewing the people of Horbury: the vicar, a bus driver, and a laborer, all figures who are performing the daily tasks which make up the lives of ordinary people. A sketch of Wakefield takes us back to 1852 and the early days of the *Express*. We are also introduced to the directors and editors of the newspaper and to the printing room. The final shot lingers on a typewriter which introduces a traveling series linking a number of news events: a rugby match, the carnival at Pontefract, the unveiling of the war memorial at Sharlston, and the welcome for a channel swimmer. Finally, there is a montage of people participating in various sorts of recreations. The camera returns to the paper and we catch a glimpse of two elderly people placing classified ads as the paper comes off the press. The film concludes by cross-cutting between the events of the day and shots of people buying, reading, and carrying the Wakefield *Express*. The final sequence of the film shows the reporter once again making his rounds collecting the news.

Notes:

Wakefield Express was made on the occasion of the newspaper's 100th anniversary. Anderson was recommended for the job by the Sutcliffes and shot the film with a budget of £600. This is the first film on which Anderson worked with John Fletcher. The film has no recorded dialogue and relies on a commentary with music and sound effects.

6. THURSDAY'S CHILDREN (1953)

Producer:	World Wide Pictures (A Morse Production)
Directors:	Guy Brenton, Lindsay Anderson
Photography:	Walter Lassally
Music:	Geoffrey Wright
Commentator:	Richard Burton
Cast:	Children from the Royal School for the Deaf, Margate, England.
Running time:	20 minutes

Synopsis

The film opens with Richard Burton's voice reciting the little poem "Monday's Child is Fair of Face" and we learn that "Thursday's Child has far to go." On the screen we see small children playing house, a young girl pouring tea, and a young boy smoking a pretend pipe and reading the newspaper. We are gradually led into the world of the deaf and the struggle that deaf children have learning to talk. We see the children at their lessons, watching their teacher's lips because they can only see or feel sounds, not hear them. Suddenly, like the children, we see her lips mouthing the words of the lesson but do not hear them. We watch as the children learn to talk by feeling the lips and throat of their teacher; we hear the children learning to speak. The teacher reads a letter from home to the children by spelling it out with words and pictures on the blackboard. They practice saying the words. We see the children acting out the story "Little Black Sambo," each taking a part and saying the words. Words grow into sentences and again we see the children struggle to say sounds they cannot "hear." The film ends with the quotation about Thursday's Child and a sequence of shots of the children, happy and playing with one another in the dining room of the school.

Notes:

This film was inspired by Guy Brenton of B.B.C. Television who asked Anderson to help him photograph the students and teachers at the Royal School for the Deaf in Margate, England. The film was started with their own money and with the help of some friends. Halfway through the production, World Wide Pictures stepped in and rescued the project financially. Quite a furor was created when it was discovered that Anderson was not a member of the cinema technician's union. It took two or three applications before the union would admit him. The film won an Oscar and was shown on Granada television in Britain and in independent cinemas, but was not distributed by a major chain. The commentary of the film, which was mainly Anderson's responsibility, was read by Richard Burton, who donated his services.

7. O DREAMLAND (1953)

Producer:	Sequence Films
Director	Lindsay Anderson
Camera:	John Fletcher
Assistant:	John Fletcher
Running time:	12 minutes

Synopsis

The initial shot is of a man polishing a Bentley. The camera pans to a crowd of people filing along a nearby street. We follow them into the amusement park, Dreamland. The film cuts to a sequence of shots in a chamber of horrors. On the sound track we hear a horrible, mechanical laughter which will periodically interrupt the film. We are shown a series of wax works scenes of torture and mutilation while the announcer tells us that "your children will love it." The next scene is of the midway with streams of people and a distorted rendition of the popular song "I Believe" in the background. We see the heavy hips of the women, the litter, and the tired faces of the crowd. We rapidly pass some caged animals, one of which is a monkey with the notice: "Warning: you touch this monkey at your own risk." The mechanical laughter introduces us to a clockwork doll rocking maniacally while a group of children watch stone-faced. In rather rapid succession we see the bingo tournament, more litter, the bingo again, and shots of the midway. "I Believe" wails in the background. A restaurant scene is introduced by the announcer who talks about the "good food" and "family atmosphere" of the "famous lunches." This spiel is interspersed with shots of people eating and overhead views of masses of baked beans and warm sausages. The film concludes with a series of shots touting the "Magic Gardens of Dreamland" with its mechanical people, recorded music, and ersatz statues. A mechanical dwarf sitting at the entrance of the gardens has a cartoon balloon which reads: "The dreams I dream are yours to see in reality over there." With "I Believe" in the background, we are shown the crowds, the mechanical figures of Sleeping Beauty and the Prince, and, finally, an aerial shot of the whole amusement park lighted at night.

Notes:

Anderson noticed this amusement park while shooting *Thursday's Children* in Margate. He made the film with only one assistant, John Fletcher, who served as his cameraman. It was shown for the first time three years later in the initial Free Cinema program at the National Film Theatre.

*8. GREEN AND PLEASANT LAND (1955)

Producer:	Leon Clore (National Society for the Prevention of Cruelty to Children), Basic Film Productions
Director:	Lindsay Anderson
Script:	Lindsay Anderson
Photography:	Walter Lassally
Running time:	4 minutes

Synopsis

This film consists of a series of tableaux of landscapes and happy children singing "Jerusalem" and still photographs of neglected children and the appalling conditions in which they live. The panning camera moves from classrooms to English landscapes. As the hymn reaches "dark and satanic mills" we are shown the other face of England, all urban squalor and industry. The images dissolve into each other as the narrator asks what sort of adults these children will become, and makes an appeal for the National Society for the Prevention of Cruelty to Children, so that it may help all such unfortunate children.

Notes:

This is the first of the films Anderson made for Leon Clore, whom he met through Clore's wife Miriam while editing *Three Installations*. This film was made as a trailer for the National Society for the Prevention of Cruelty to Children (NSPCC).

*9. HENRY (1955)

Producer:	Leon Clore (National Society for the Prevention of Cruelty to Children), Basic Film Productions
Director:	Lindsay Anderson
Script:	Lindsay Anderson
Photography:	Walter Lassally
Running time:	5½ minutes

Synopsis

This straightforward narrative tells the story of Henry, an eight-year-old boy who runs away from home while his parents are having a fight. The film cuts to the Picadilly Underground sign and then crosscuts back and forward through a montage of sights and sound of the circus: sex shops, neon signs, crowds, shop windows, film posters, newspaper sellers, litter-strewn pavements, and, finally, to close-ups of Henry who is taking all this in. Henry steals some money from a man and experiences his first cigarette. He is also offered a sweet by a stranger. He makes his way to a railroad station, with the intention of traveling even farther from his parents, when he is apprehended by a friendly ticket collector who calls in an NSPCC inspector.

Notes:

This is the second in the dramas Anderson did for the NSPCC. Anderson spotted the central character of this film, a pensive small boy, from among those who sang for *Green and Pleasant Land.* This film was shot entirely at night and was the first film to use new fast stock, Ilford H.P.S. Anderson plays a small role as the NSPCC officer who rescues Henry.

*10. THE CHILDREN UPSTAIRS (1955)

Producer:	Leon Clore (National Society for the Prevention of Cruelty to Children), Basic Film Productions
Director:	Lindsay Anderson
Script:	Lindsay Anderson
Photography:	Walter Lassally
Running time:	4 minutes

Synopsis

A neighbor calls in the NSPCC inspector to talk about her fears for the welfare of the children upstairs. The inspector makes his first visit in plain clothes, and listens to the neighbor's story of the neglected children. Having assured the woman that the Society's policy is not to divulge the sources of their information, he leaves, only to return to the house in uniform to meet the mother and her children. He finds typically neglected children in filthy conditions and begins to try to help the mother with her difficulties.

Notes:

This is the third of the Society's films. It reflects Anderson's interest in the Italian neo-realists.

*11. A HUNDRED THOUSAND CHILDREN (1955)

Producer:	Leon Clore (National Society for the Prevention of Cruelty to Children), Basic Film Production
Director:	Lindsay Anderson
Script:	Lindsay Anderson
Photography:	Walter Lassally
Running time:	4 minutes

Synopsis

An appeal made by Ann Allen opens with shots of newspaper cuttings showing stories of neglected and ill-treated children, and states that every year 100,000 children are helped by the Society. The film continues with an inspector relating his experiences with cases and how the Society has helped the children involved.

Notes:

This was the fourth and last of the trailers Anderson shot for the society.

*12. £20 A TON (1955)

Producer:	Leon Clore (National Industrial Fuel Efficiency Serice), Basic Film Production
Director:	Lindsay Anderson
Photography:	Larry Pizer
Production Manager:	John Fletcher
Running time:	approximately 5 minutes

Synopsis

A business man is conducted around his factory and shown every leak of steam, every gap through which heat could escape, and is made to realize how each of these adds to the price of coal. It is worked out that, as a result of his inefficiencies, he pays £20 for a ton of coal.

Notes:

This was meant to be a humorous treatment of fuel wastage. The price of £20 a ton for coal was apparently a steep one for the time.

*13. ENERGY FIRST (1955)

Producer:	Leon Clore (National Industrial Fuel Efficiency Service), Basic Film Production
Director:	Lindsay Anderson
Photography:	Larry Pizer
Production Manager:	John Fletcher
Running time:	approximately 5 minutes

Notes:

Anderson has absolutely no recollection of *Energy First*.

14. FOOT AND MOUTH (1955)

Producer:	Leon Clore (Central Office of Information for the Ministry of Agriculture, Fisheries, and Food), Basic Film Production
Director:	Lindsay Anderson
Script:	Lindsay Anderson
Photography:	Walter Lassally
Editor:	Bill Megarry
Technical Advisor:	J. C. Davidson, M.R.C.V.S.
Production Manager:	Philip Aizlewood
Commentator:	Lindsay Anderson
Running time:	20 minutes

Synopsis

The tractor which has been plowing during the credits enters a farmyard as the narrator introduces the two young farmers who are the focus of this film. The camera takes in various details of the farmyard, animals, grain sacks, and the like. The two farmers, the Harding brothers, are requested by the cowman to examine one of their cows which is to be shipped to market. After looking at the cow, the brothers decide to keep her from market but ship the others, instead. The narrator asks if it was really wise to send the others on. A montage follows showing various sick animals and aborted calves and lambs while the narrator catalogues the symptoms and causes of hoof and mouth disease. The narrator describes how the disease can spread rapidly from animal to animal, infecting herds over a wide area. Meanwhile, we see the cows being sold at market and the veterinarian visiting "Bury Farms" and posting a quarantine sign. A veterinarian is seen examining more animals and finally destroying some. The sequence concludes with a shot of deserted pastures. The narrator outlines the outbreak of the disease during 1951-1952. On a map of England the spread of the earlier epidemic is graphically depicted. A map of Europe reveals the outbreak of similar epidemics on the Continent. Finally the whole world is shown.

The disease is very contagious, and in a series of vignettes we are shown how simple acts of carelessness can lead to the spread of hoof and mouth disease. A dog finds a bone from an infected animal and carries it home, thereby infecting another farm. The narrator explains what the Harding brothers should have done when they first noticed the infected animal and what precautions were called for to protect the neighboring herds. The farm is completely disinfected. Following another montage of sick animals and aborted lambs and calves, we see the farmer carefully examining a sick cow. The film concludes with David Harding looking puzzled and the narrator saying that suspicion is enough to warrant reporting any disease.

Notes:

Anderson did the narration on this film, which is a marvel of indirection, since no outbreaks of the disease actually were occurring at the time of the shooting. Once again, Lassally did the camera work and Anderson did the script. The film was made for Leon Clore at the Central Office of Information for the Ministry of Agriculture. The two young farmers who appear in this film actually owned the farm, located just north of Edgware and used as the central location of the movie.

15. EVERY DAY EXCEPT CHRISTMAS (1957)

Producers:	Leon Clore, Karel Reisz (Ford of Britain), A Graphic Film
Director:	Lindsay Anderson
Photography:	Walter Lassally
Music:	Daniel Paris
Recording:	John Fletcher
Sound Editing:	John Fletcher
Assistants:	Alex Jacobs, Brian Probyn, Maurice Ammar
Commentator:	Alun Owen
Running time:	40 minutes

Synopsis

The film begins with several workers loading mushrooms, roses, and lettuce onto a truck in a market garden in Sussex. At midnight the truck pulls out on its way to London and we hear the BBC Light Programme closing for the night. As "God Save the Queen" plays over the radio, a prolonged tracking shot carries the truck past country roads, through the darkened streets of deserted villages and residential suburbs, and into London itself. The commentary which takes over from the anthem mentions the wide diversity of the foodstuffs coming to the market from all over Britain: apples from Kent, potatoes from Norfolk, and oranges and lemons from the western ports. The tracking shot ends with a still shot of the empty market and the words: "All these roads lead to London," A stationary shot of a deserted alley is animated by a whistling porter who is soon joined by others who fill up the screen with activity. The pace quickens with a series of short takes which introduce the variety of jobs the market requires, setting up the displays and unloading boxes and sacks, and the general activity in the streets around the market itself. We see the truck driver from Sussex drinking tea while his truck is being unloaded of its mushrooms, lettuce, and roses. The camera now begins to follow some of the people in the market and to probe into the various areas of their activity. Again we see in a series of short takes the variety of jobs going on in the preparation of the stalls. A worker whistles a ditty. At 4:30 a.m., after the displays have been set up for the day, the workers go off for a tea break. Again we see the empty market, but the camera pans with some of the workers as they enter a cafe, "Albert's," and the next sequence is shot inside it as we see the men relaxing after the hours of work. Both the night workers and the habitués of the night mingle in the cafe, chatting, eating, drinking tea and coffee, and listening to the radio. In another series of shots Anderson compiles a record of the people inside. The whole of this series is covered by the music coming from the jukebox. The music stops and we are again subjected to a shift of mood as we see a display of tulips and shots of persons nodding off or resting after the morning's work. The film concludes with the arrival of a street band and the hustle to get the vegetables to the shops by nine o'clock. The buyers come to the market to shop for fashionable London stores, restaurant owners purchase food to be prepared, and flower sellers buy their daily stock. Porters wheel the goods to waiting trucks which haul them away. The market workers return to "Albert's" for more tea and sausages. The pace slackens and by 10:30 a.m. a lull occurs and we see a woman porter putting her feet up and a man putting his boxes away for another day. Finally the old ladies who sell flowers on the streets arrive to get their wares. Once again the trucks travel, but this time outward from London back into the countryside. The narrator notes that the market has been there for 300 years and, although it has changed, it remains the same. The market has come to represent the interdependence of the working man. The film ends with a series of smiles and a closeup of one of the porters laughing into the camera.

Notes:

Anderson had the opportunity to make *Every Day Except Christmas* because of Karel Reisz, who had been making commercial films for the Ford Motor Company with the understanding that they would finance a series of documentaries not based on advertising Ford products. Anderson was asked by Reisz to do the first film. He began with the idea of a film on the catching, loading, and transporting of fish throughout Britain. Then there was a project to make a film for the BBC about long distance truck drivers but this fell through. Finally Anderson began on the Covent Garden film. Most of the film was improvised on the spot and the shooting was followed by five months of editing. The film is dedicated to "Alice and George and Bill and Sid and Alan and George and Derek and Bill and all the others ...." The movie was rejected initially by the British selection board for the Venice Film Festival, but later won the Grand Prix.

16. THIS SPORTING LIFE (1963)

Producer:	Karel Reisz (A Julian Wintle/Leslie Parkyn Production)
Director:	Lindsay Anderson
Screenplay:	David Storey, based on his novel, *This Sporting Life*
Photography:	Denys Coop
Camera Operator:	John Harris
Art Direction:	Alan Withy
Set Dresser:	Peter Lamont
Music Composer:	Roberto Gerhard
Music Conductor:	Jacques-Louis Monod
Sound Editor:	Chris Greenham
Sound Recording:	John W. Mitchell, Gordon K. McCallum
Dress Designer:	Sophie Devine
Editor:	Peter Taylor
Assistant Editor:	Tom Priestley
Assistant Director:	Ted Sturgis
In Charge of Production:	Albert Fennell
Production Manager:	Geoffrey Haine
Continuity:	Pamela Mann
Casting:	Miriam Brickman
Make-up:	Bob Lawrence
Hairdressing:	Ivy Emmerton
Properties:	Ernie Quick
Cast:	Richard Harris (Frank Machin), Rachel Roberts (Mrs. Hammond), Alan Badel (Weaver), William Hartnell (Johnson), Colin Blakely (Maurice Braithwaite), Vanda Godsell (Mrs. Weaver), Arthur Lowe (Sloamer), Anne Cunningham (Judith), Jack Watson (Len Miller), Harry Markham (Wade), George Sewell (Jeff), Leonard Rossiter (Phillips), Frank Windsor (Dentist), Peter Dugoid (Doctor), Wallas Eaton (Waiter), Anthony Woodruff (Head Waiter), Katherine Parr (Mrs. Farrer), Bernadette Benson (Lynda), Andrew Nolan (Ian), Michael Logan (Riley), Murray Evans (Hooker), Tom Clegg (Gower), John Gill (Cameron), Ken Traill (Trainer).
Running time:	134 minutes

Synopsis

A violent scene during a rugby match opens the film. We hear and see the grunting men and the smack as they hit each other. Frank Machin is hit in the mouth. His injury is obviously a foul, very much like the one he committed earlier on another play and which we will see later on in the film. From a subjective shot while he is lying on his back looking up at the trainer, we flash back to his earlier life as a coal miner. It is only momentary. The next series of shots flash backward to his life with his landlady, Mrs. Hammond, and then to various scenes in the locker room as footballers clean up after the game. He is taken from the jocular locker room atmosphere to the sterile atmosphere of the dentist's office.

In the dentist's chair, as he breathes in the gas, the film goes into flashback, this time filling in more about Frank and his landlady. We see the antagonism between the two, one bitter and the other trying too hard. Periodically there are flash-forwards to Frank sitting in the chair. The second major flashback shows Frank at an earlier period before he played football. He crashes into a dance hall on the heels of the city's rugby league team. He sees the adulation they receive and deliberately picks a fight with the captain of the team. He waits for the team's scout to leave and asks him to get him a trial. In the trial game Frank plays with unusual savagery and during scrum he fouls one of his own men who has refused to allow him to score. Machin's hard play impresses the owners of the team.

In the paper the following day, he reads about his performance in the game. He has been singled out for praise by the sportswriter. He tears out the clipping and shares it with Johnson, the scout, who has accompanied him home. Mrs. Hammond arrives and Machin and the woman discuss the rugby team after Johnson leaves. As Frank sits and reads, Mrs. Hammond kneels by the fire and polishes her dead husband's boots which she keeps on the fender. During this scene she confesses her guilt about her treatment of her husband and we see Machin's obvious infatuation with her. Frank retires upstairs and puts his clipping on his mirror before he poses in front of it.

Next we watch as Frank negotiates with the board, demanding a thousand pounds to sign with the team. He drives a hard bargain, but the board decides to meet his offer. Amid congratulations he is given a check for the thousand. Weaver, one of the owners, drives him home and confesses that Mrs. Hammond's husband, one of his workers, may have killed himself.

Machin meets Johnson outside his lodging and after teasing him, impresses him with the size of the check, and he offers him some of it for his help. His announcement that the team has signed him does not impress Mrs. Hammond, but she mellows when he tells her how much they gave him. She quickly notes that it is more than she got when her husband died. Machin slams out of the house. Later we see him lying in bed reading a book called *Cry Tough*, with the check propped on the night stand beside him.

The film flashes forward again into the present as Frank is carried from the dentist's, still reacting from the gas. He mutters, "She gives me nothing, bloody nothing." One of the owners drives him home, which leads to another flashback to Frank standing in front of the house showing his new car to Mrs. Hammond. The film then flashes forward to the Christmas party given by Weaver for the team, where Frank is cheered as he arrives. The party is now in full swing and Frank wanders through it, a little dazed, exchanging greetings with the other players. Upstairs he washes his face and inspects his wounded mouth. He sits on a bed, which occasions another flashback. This time he is taking Mrs. Hammond and her children for a day in the country. During this pastoral interlude Frank and the children play together and after enough kidding, Mrs. Hammond smiles and joins in briefly with their games. She seems to enjoy his playing with the children and actually laughs when he wades in to fetch the ball he has kicked into the river.

The film cuts to a montage of shots of another rugby game showing Frank scoring goals and the happy faces of the owners. After the game, Weaver's wife asks to be introduced to Machin. He goes to a nightclub where, with one of his teammates, they meet a couple of girls. Frank agrees to sing a song for the amateur night. Slightly off key, he sings "Here in My Heart" which entrances the audience. He returns rather drunk to his lodging and has a scene with Mrs. Hammond. The next morning he is lying on his bed brooding when Mrs. Hammond comes in to clean up his room. He grabs her and throws her on the bed. She fights him and they are interrupted by her daughter outside the door. The mother sends her away.

We next see Machin in the pub, the center of attention as he recites his exploits on the field. He has become boisterous and loud. He plays the game for the fans, he says. He boasts about his invitation to join Mrs. Weaver at home for drinks. He goes to the Weavers' and she invites him to their Christmas Eve party. He is obviously nervous with her and paces the living room like a caged animal. When she kisses him he bolts, remarking that it wouldn't be fair to her husband. The film flashes forward once again to Frank on the bed upstairs at the party, and then back again to Frank and Mrs. Hammond on his bed together. She calls him a stupid animal and the film flashes forward to the party again.

He wanders through the party and stumbles into Weaver's room where the owners are having drinks. They humiliate him. It is obvious that neither of the Weavers wants him around anymore. Sloamer, another of the owners, gets him outside and warns him about Weaver. He returns to the party to see the team singing "For He's a Jolly Good Fellow" to Weaver. He wanders alone through the streets carrying his bag of Christmas presents for the family, arriving home to find Mrs. Hammond decorating for the next day. She reminisces about her girlhood. She is genuinely concerned when she notices his mouth and goes to bed with him, "just for Christmas night."

Machin takes Mrs. Hammond out for dinner but embarrasses her by giving her a fur coat to wear. She is concerned about what the neighbors will say. The scene at a posh restaurant shows Frank acting like a boor in front of Mrs. Hammond and the other diners, who include the Weavers. He is ill-at-ease in these surroundings. He announces to her that he knows how to handle these people. Finally Mrs. Hammond is so embarrassed that she leaves him sitting at the table. As he leaves he says hello to the Weavers, who ignore him completely.

It is Easter time and Frank and Mrs. Hammond are attending his friend's wedding. In the churchyard afterward, Mrs. Hammond confesses that she is ashamed of their relationship. It stuns Frank and he hits her when she says that she feels like dirt. He learns later that the whole street thinks him a joke, a great ape who performs on Saturday. Later, she throws him out of the house after he demands that she acknowledge that she needs him. He confesses his confusion to his just-married friend at a pub. He admits that she makes him want to crush everything. He says he wants something permanent.

Back at the house he suggests that she see a doctor after the fainting spell she experienced when they were quarreling earlier. She refuses. He berates her memory of her husband in order to win her away from him. He tells her of his suspicion of her husband's suicide. In a rage he admits that he needs her. She begs him to leave her alone. He declares his love for her, but she remains adamant and asks him to leave. As he wanders the hills outside the town, we see a montage of rugby players wallowing in the muck of a playing field. In slow motion we see him exhausted on the field.

He races from the flop house where he is now living back to Mrs. Hammond's, only to learn that she has been taken ill and is in the hospital. Frank learns that she has had a brain hemorrhage and that it is dangerous because she apparently hasn't the will to live. He tries to talk her comatose body into living. He mutters over and over again that she is all right, that she can't leave him. Spotting a spider on the wall, he leans up to smash it when she suddenly begins to bleed at the mouth and dies. He refuses to believe the doctor when he tells him that she is dead. Seeing the spider on the wall again he screams "No!" and smashes it with his fist.

Frank wanders out of the hospital and crashes back into the house where he desolately prowls the rooms until he falls to his knees sobbing. The closing scene is composed of a series of shots, many of them in slow motion, of another rugby game. Machin, tired, trots off the field to join his team.

Notes:

Anderson became interested in David Storey's novel as a possible film project in 1960 when it was first published. The directorial job was initially offered to Karel Reisz by Julian Wintle and Leslie Parkyn of Independent Artists, who had bought the property when it proved too costly for Woodfall Films. Reisz told them that he would rather try his hand at producing and suggested Anderson be hired as the director, instead. The script was put together by Anderson and Storey, with the help of Richard Harris. Harris won the grand prize at the Cannes festival in 1963 for his portrayal of Frank Machin.

*17. THE WHITE BUS (1967)[3]

Executive Producer: Oscar Lewenstein (United Artists), A Woodfall Films Presentation.
Associate Producer: Michael Deeley
Director: Lindsay Anderson
Screenplay: Shelagh Delaney, based on an original story by Shelagh Delaney
Photography: Miroslav Ondricek
Editor: Kevin Brownlow
Art Director: David Marshall

Music: Misha Donat
Sound Editor: John Fletcher
Sound Recorder: Peter Handford
Casting Director: Miriam Brickman
Assistant Director: Kip Gowans
Production
  Manager: Jake Wright
Cast: Patricia Healey (Girl), Arthur Lowe (Mayor), John
                     Sharp (Macebearer), Julie Perry (Bus
                     Conductress), Victor Henry ("Transistorite"), Stephen
                     Moore (Smart Young Man), Fanny Carby (Football
                     Supporter), Anthony Hopkins (Brechtian Singer),
                     Jeanne Watts (Fish-and-Chip Shop Woman), Alaba
                     Peters, Ronald Lacey, Margaret Barron.
Running time: 46 minutes

Synopsis

The film opens with a shot of a boy on a barge on the Thames, then a shot of an office building, and finally a shot of a girl working late at her typewriter in a modern office while some cleaners work around her. There is a sudden cut to the girl hanging from the ceiling, but the cleaners go on with their work as if nothing has happened. The girl hurries along a railway station platform to catch a train. She is pursued by her suitor in his city dress who shouts his willingness to mate with her, denying the existence of a class barrier. As the train pulls out of the station, he falls on his knees and bursts into song. The train is full of football fans from the north of England who sing to establish their community solidarity, a scene which contrasts sharply with the next one in which the girl finds herself alone in the quiet streets of her once-familiar hometown. She sees a woman, whose isolated footsteps dominate the soundtrack, as she is abducted by two men who bundle her into a car and drive away. We see animals being led to slaughter and a young man running past her in a jogging outfit.

A great deal of the film is spent on the official tour of the town on the white bus, a scene which is dominated by the mayor's official unctuousness. The bus is inhabited by the well-meaning conductress who monotonously recites the facts and figures about the town, a group of councillors, and a number of tourists in their national costumes: a Japanese woman, a bowler-wearing English businessman, a Nigerian man, and the local mace-bearer who goes around with the mayor. We are given a series of shots juxtaposing the flaccid faces of tired middle-aged women with stuffed apes in the museum, and the visual contrasts of modern blocks of buildings with the parkland which surrounds a once stately home. The richness of the local industry (pottery, tapestry, cakes) and the local cultural institutions (public library, museum, art gallery) are all suggested on the bus tour. Finally, the passengers are all turned into manikins while watching a civil defense demonstration, leaving the girl alone to watch the proceedings.

In the concluding sequences the girl abandons the tourists and wanders through the lamplit streets at twilight. Behind the windows she sees shots of a girl playing the piano and an old woman shaving an old man. She also witnesses a scene where a boy is trying to seduce a girl in an alley and, after frightening the girl off by his eagerness, vents his frustration on the heroine. She finally ends up at a fish-and-chips shop at closing time, where an assistant recites a speech about how routine and repetitive work is from day to day as he stacks the chairs on the tables.

Notes:

The White Bus was originally to be one of a trilogy of films made for Woodfall called *Red, White, and Zero.* Oscar Lewenstein suggested that each of the three Free Cinema directors, Anderson, Reisz, and Richardson, do a short film. When *Morgan: A Suitable Case for Treatment* by Reisz ran to feature length, Peter Brook was brought in to replace him. At an early stage of the project, Richardson wanted to do *Pavan for a Dead Princess* based on a short story by Shelagh Delaney. It was then that Lewenstein proposed that the trilogy should be made up of three Delaney short stories, and Anderson was given *The White Bus.* Richardson made a short called *Red and Blue,* based on three songs and starring Vanessa Redgrave. Peter Brook directed *The Ride of the Valkyries,* a film starring Zero Mostel. The final three films lacked any continuity so the trilogy was never released as such.

Anderson meanwhile worked with Delaney, who did the script, and completed *The White Bus.* It was two years after the completion of the film before it was shown publicly in Britain, and then only for a brief stint at a South Kensington cinema with Vera Chytilova's *Daisies.*

18. RAZ DWA TRZY (The Singing Lesson) (1967)

Producer:	Miroslaw Podolski (Contemporary Films), Warsaw Documentary Studios.
Director:	Lindsay Anderson
Photography:	Zygmunt Samosiuk
Editor:	Barbara Kosidowska
Song Arrangement:	Ludwik Sempolinski
Piano Accompaniment:	Irena Klukowna
Sound Editor:	Henryk Kuzniak
Sound Recorder:	Malgorzata Jaworska
Assistant Director:	Joanna Nawrocka
Singers:	Piotr Fronczewski ("The Coat"), Anita Przysiecka, Marian Glinka ("Big Beat"), Aniceta Raczek ("A Lullaby—for those who wait"), Waldemar Walisiak ("Sunshine Street"), Andrzej Nardelli ("Sweet Peas"), Joanna Sobieska, Andrzej Seweryn ("Oh, Miss Sabina!").
Running time:	20 minutes

Synopsis

The film opens with a clapper-board in front of the stage on which the students from the Warsaw Dramatic Academy are rehearsing songs. The first song, "The Coat," does not begin in the classroom but rather with a shot of a train pulling into a station. During the song the film cuts back and forth between crowds at the station, street scenes, buildings, memorials, and images of war—empty bowls, a photograph of a man with sad eyes, and a list of names and dates—to close-ups of the students and teachers watching the rehearsal. As the title suggests, the song is about Poland's inheritance, of "the winds of history that buffet its people." The point of view within the class shifts from the boy who is singing to the piano player, to the class with the professor, and back to the boy. We are momentarily distracted by a student who arrives late as we watch him remove his coat and sit down with the others.

The second song, "Big Beat," is sung by a boy in a checked shirt and a girl in a mini-skirt and boots. This time the film moves outside the classroom to photograph patterns of umbrellas on a rainy day. We watch a cloakroom attendant hang up coats on racks. The third song, "A Lullaby—for those who wait," which is sung by a girl, involves cutting back and forth between the class and shots of women waiting in shops. We see a customer in a china shop staring blankly and shopgirls waiting patiently. In a souvenir shop a woman looks directly into the camera. There is a brief but memorable shot of a man sleeping in a station waiting room. The contrast with the animated girl singer is vivid.

The fourth song, "Sunshine Street," is about those middle-class people who are waited on by shop assistants, but the song is livelier and the shoppers are obviously better off than the ones from the previous segment. This segment opens with the shot of a tree in a fashionable shopping section of the city. We see three women trying on hats and coats in department stores. It is a section full of mirrors and beautifully made-up women. The three women end the song eating ice cream in a fashionable restaurant. The fifth song, sung by a boy, is called "Sweet Peas" and is a song from a gardener's boy to his lover. The opening shot is of a cat, after which the camera never leaves the classroom, but alternates between the singer and the various girls in the room. We see in close-up the girl's reactions to the singer.

The sixth and final song, "Oh, Miss Sabina," begins in the classroom with a dialogue between two students in antique costume. The professor interrupts the song a couple of times to show the boy how his part should be played. The camera focuses on the students and the piano accompanist as they react to the singing and directing. Then there is a short interlude with a speeded up sequence. The professor begins to dance with one of the women students and soon everyone in the room is dancing. The music carries the viewer out over the city of Warsaw to observe the tired faces of the rush hour crowds as they hurry home after the day's work. The camera follows one particular pedestrian who is carrying a small bunch of daffodils.

Notes:

Anderson made this film at the invitation of the Warsaw Documentary Studios while he was in Poland directing Tadeusz Lomnicki in a production of John Osborne's "Inadmissible Evidence" at the Contemporary Theatre during the 1966 season. Anderson had been impressed by Lomnicki's performance in Andrzej Wajda's film, *A Generation,* which he had seen at the Cannes Film Festival in 1957, and which he was covering for *Sight and Sound* (*See* no. 41). Apparently Anderson met Lomnicki when he visited Poland for the BBC about that time. Lomnicki originally wanted Anderson to direct him in a production of "Hamlet," but later a more contemporary drama was chosen. The subject of *The Singing Lesson* arose when Anderson's assistant at the Contemporary Theatre took him to visit the acting class of Professor Ludwik Simpolinski at the Warsaw Dramatic Academy. In the afternoon of his visit to the class of third-year students, Anderson saw three of the songs featured in the film. He made the film in 1967 using the same students. The film took about three weeks to shoot and was filmed by a young Polish cameraman, Zygmunt Samosiuk.

19. **IF...** (1969)

Producer:	Michael Medwin, Lindsay Anderson (Paramount), A Memorial Enterprises Film
Director:	Lindsay Anderson
Screenplay:	David Sherwin, from the original script "Crusaders" by David Sherwin and John Howlett
Director of Photography	Miroslav Ondricek
Cameraman:	Chris Menges
Camera Operator:	Brian Harris
Camera Assistant:	Michael Seresin
Editor:	David Gladwell
Assistant Editors:	Ian Rakoff, Michael Ellis
Production Designer:	Jocelyn Herbert
Wardrobe:	Shura Cohen
Music:	Composed and conducted by Marc Wilkinson, "Sanctus" from the "Missa Luba" (Philips recording).
Dubbing Editor:	Alan Bell
Dubbing Mixer:	Doug Turner
Sound Recordist:	Christian Wangler
Casting Director:	Miriam Brickman
Assistant Director:	John Stoneman
Production Manager:	Gavrik Losey
Assistant to Producer:	Neville Thompson
Assistants to Director:	Stephen Frears, Stuart Baird
Continuity:	Valerie Booth
Make-up:	Betty Blattner
Construction Manager:	Jack Carter

Cast: Crusaders—Malcolm McDowell (Mick), David Wood
                    (Johnny), Richard Warwick (Wallace), Christine
                    Noonan (Girl), Rupert Webster (Bobby Philips);
                    Whips—Robert Swann (Rowntree), Hugh Thomas
                    (Denson), Michael Cadman (Fortinbras), Peter Sproule
                    (Barnes); Staff—Peter Jeffrey (Headmaster), Arthur
                    Lowe (Mr. Kemp), Mona Washbourne (Matron), Mary
                    MacLeod (Mrs. Kemp), Geoffrey Chater (Chaplain),
                    Ben Aris (John Thomas), Graham Crowden (History
                    Master), Charles Lloyd Pack (Classics Master),
                    Anthony Nicholls (General Denson), Tommy Godfrey
                    (Finchley); Seniors—Guy Ross (Stephans), Robin
                    Askwith (Keating), Richard Everett (Pussy Graves),
                    Philip Bagenal (Peanuts), Nicholas Page (Cox), Robert
                    Yetzes (Fisher), David Griffen (Willens), Graham
                    Sharman (Van Eyssen), Richard Tombleson (Baird);
                    Juniors—Richard Davis (Machin), Brian Pettifer
                    (Biles), Michael Newport (Brunning), Charles
                    Sturridge (Markland), Sean Bury (Jute), Martin
                    Beaumont (Hunter).
Running time: 112 minutes

Synopsis

With boys' voices singing the college song in the background, the film
opens on a title containing a quotation from Proverbs (4:7):

> Wisdom is the principal thing;
> therefore get wisdom;
> and with all thy getting
> get understanding.

As the boys continue to sing, the credits roll over a sepia print of the
college as seen in near silhouette from the playing fields. The music stops
and is replaced by the sound of commotion: running, banging, shouting, and
giggling. The print of the college fades and is replaced by the title "College
House:... return." The scene opens onto a corridor crowded with boys
carrying trunks, sporting equipment, and boxes of foodstuffs. The corridor
is chaotic. Rowntree, one of the school prefects or whips, suddenly calls out,
"Run in the corridor!" and the boys run. Jute, a new boy or scum, is
introduced and we follow him through his initiation into the school's
mysteries. Brunning is assigned as Jute's tutor, and he takes Jute around the
school to find him a spare desk and in general to acquaint him with the new
environment. Jute is told that he may not have tinned food except fruits and
beans without meat. The whole process is one of urgency and confusion.

Mick arrives wearing a hat and is muffled up to his eyes in a scarf.
Someone says, "It's Guy Fawkes back again." Mick's friends Johnny and
Wallace make fun of Stephans, who is trying to get order from the returning
boys. Mick dives into his study and unwraps his scarf, revealing a
moustache. Johnny is a little in awe of it. Mick begins to shave it off almost
as soon as he unwraps it. Johnny inspects the contents of Mick's trunk while
he shaves. Johnny confesses that he built a hut in the woods over the

vacation; Mick says that he met this girl and went around to all the pubs. The boys are assembled in the dining room for medical inspection and a welcome from the housemaster. Mr. Kemp tells the boys to remember just one rule, "Work—play—but don't mix the two." The camera pans the staff assembled at the head of the hall with the master while the speeches go on. Rowntree, the senior whip, announces that there is not going to be a continuation of the deplorable lack of spirit exhibited during the summer term. The section ends with dormitory inspection by the senior whips. They admonish Mick to get his hair cut and congratulate Stephans on the condition of the dorm. Mick and Johnny and Wallace razz Stephans as soon as the whips leave and in the dark, after the lights have been extinguished, the boys continue to banter among themselves.

The second section of the film begins with the title "College: Once again assembled...." The camera pans the boys, masters, and other college domestics as they sit in the chapel. After the service we see the headmaster lecturing the whips outside, and in general spreading an atmosphere of congenial authority. The film cuts to the upper form students sitting in a classroom when suddenly the history master, while singing a hymn, comes cycling into the class. He passes out the holiday papers, banters about the term's direction, and then assigns an essay. We next see Jute in a mathematics class conducted by the chaplain, who walks around the room smacking and pinching the boys. The headmaster is lecturing the whips on the parade ground as the ROTC troops march in the background. His speech is full of empty platitudes about middle-class moral values which are indispensable in the modern age. Jute is being tutored for his examination of the master's names. Biles, the butt of many of the boy's sadistic jokes, is dragged into the toilet and suspended head down over one of them. Wallace, who has been sitting in one of the cubicles during the escapade, releases him. Stephans confesses to the chaplain that he is having dirty thoughts and is admonished to "fight the good fight."

The third part, "Term Time," opens with a shot of Mr. Thomas, the new teacher, coaching the boys in rugby. After a brief scene with the matron dispensing clean shirts and collars, the film switches to the senior prefects' room where they are discussing the beauty of Rowntree's fag, Phillips. Rowntree gives him to Denson. Wallace, Johnny, and Mick are in Wallace's study where they discuss violence, rebellion, naked girls, and bad breath. Denson arrives and catches them drinking and sentences them to cold showers the next day. The next morning Phillips shaves Denson and fetches him tea as Wallace, Johnny, and Mick endure their cold showers. Denson makes Mick stay in much longer than the others.

Section four, "Ritual and Romance," begins with another chapel scene where Rowntree reads from the Bible as the camera pans the boys and staff. Barnes is next shown helping the boys with gymnastics. After the exercise the junior boys get their sweaters and Phillips spots Wallace doing his exercise on the high bar. The film goes to rose tint as in slow motion Wallace performs his rhythmic exercises. Phillips, obviously entranced, looks on from above. The lyric quality of the scene is broken by Barnes, who tells the boys to get back to their houses, and the film returns to regular speed and color. Next, Mick, Wallace, and Johnny are in the gym dueling with swords, shouting all sorts of romantic dialogue from adventure stories: "Death to tyrants," and "Who dies if freedom lives." The lark stops when Mick is scratched by one of the swords and shows the blood, "real blood," to his friends. Johnny, Wallace, and Mick are at the table in the dining hall. They quietly and politely torment Mrs. Kemp, the housemaster's wife, who sits with them. Rowntree announces that cheering at college matches will increase and that everyone will attend the match that afternoon and cheer loudly. At the match, while everyone else is cheering loudly, Mick and Johnny slip off to town where they perform antics on the street until they steal a motorbike from a showroom and drive into the country. They stop at an inn where they encounter a sultry waitress. Mick teases her, and is insolent and coyly sexual. He puts money into the jukebox and to the tune of "Missa Luba," the girl and Mick suddenly are rolling on the floor completely naked, growling and spitting like big cats. The scene abruptly changes as the threesome are shown playing the children's game paper-and-scissors at the table. The section ends with the girl standing on the back of the motorbike as the boys drive over green fields with the Missa Luba in the background.

"Discipline" is the title of the fifth section of the film which begins with a montage of evening activities: Mr. Thomas working on his car, being admonished by Denson about lights-out; and Phillips and Wallace smoking in the armory, talking about Phillips' divorced parents until Denson catches them. Wallace lets Phillips get away and will not tell Denson who was with him. The three rebels talk about the most horrible way to die. The four whips sit around the table in the housemaster's private dining room and discuss discipline. Kemp quizzes the whips about the state of the school. Mick, Johnny, and Wallace are called into Rowntree's study and are told they are to be beaten for their general attitude. Denson tries to make the three more obedient and Mick tells Rowntree off. In the next scene, the three boys are beaten in the gym, one at a time while the others wait outside. The punishment is done with excruciating slowness and Mick is given an especially brutal caning. The scene and the section end with the traditional thank-you delivered by the chastised boy to the one who has disciplined him. Mick shakes Rowntree's hand.

The next sequence is titled "Resistance." It opens in a Latin class but cuts quickly to Mick in his study shooting darts at the various pictures on his study wall, most of them representing middle-class life or traditional values. Rowntree rouses College House by announcing that they have won a memorial chalice. They cheer. Mick, Wallace, and Johnny drink in the study and announce that they are alone now in this rebellion. They form a blood brothership, and as they clasp bleeding hands announce: "Death to the oppressors!" "Liberty!" and "The Resistance!" Mick then discloses he has real bullets for the ROTC exercises. The film cuts to Kemp and his wife in their bedroom. He sings while she accompanies him on a recorder. The section closes as Peanuts tells Mick about the expanding of the universe and they look through his telescope at the stars.

The next to the last section, "Forth to War," begins again in the chapel with the chaplain preaching on the crime of betrayal and desertion. The next montage of the boys in uniform ready for their field days is briefly interrupted by the headmaster's wife wandering naked through the dorm. The montage continues as the boys take objectives and otherwise carry on in a military fashion. Peanuts teaches the little boys the yell of hate they are supposed to use when they charge with their bayonets. The exercises come to an end when the school stops for tea. The quiet, however, is broken as bullets rip through the tea urn, and scatter the boys behind their trucks. The chaplain approaches the three rebels, demanding that they surrender their arms. We see Mick give the yell of hate and plunge his bayonet into the cringing, begging chaplain. A cut is made to the headmaster's study where he reveals the chaplain in a large drawer in the sideboard and makes the boys apologize to him. He then gives the boys some constructive work to make up for their transgressions, not a punishment but a chance to serve. Wallace, Johnny, Mick, and Phillips are cleaning out bric-a-brac from under the stage of the lecture hall. The boys cart out a variety of things to be burned or thrown away. They discover a fetus in a jar of a cabinet. The boys look at it with wonder and the girl suddenly appears. Together the five of them discover a cache of World War II armaments. The scene and this section end as the rebels break open the cases of ammunition and pass the items around to one another.

The final section, "Crusaders," begins on honors day with the arrival of General Denson who is to give a speech. As the camera pans the assembled guests and students, a chorus sings the college song in the background. The headmaster begins his brief remarks after the ceremonial greeting of an old boy dressed in a knight's outfit. He introduces General Denson who launches into his hearty and rather platitudinous remarks. The camera alternates between the dias and the audience. Slowly, smoke begins to seep up through the floor boards under the General's feet. At first he does not notice it but finally, the hall in panic, he realizes what is going on and tries to restore order. A high angle shot from outside reveals the guests and students pouring out of the hall onto the green courtyard. Suddenly there is an explosion and parents and students fall to the ground. A low angle shot of the roof of a nearby building reveals Mick firing a Sten gun into the fleeing mob below. The girl feeds him magazines for the gun as he fires. What follows is a montage of the rebels dressed in World War II gear firing from above, and the school below, which arms and begins to fire back. The general organizes the ROTC as the bishop and parents and students take cover. The rebels continue to pour a fusillade of fire onto the quadrangle below. The camera closes in on Mick, and with a stationary shot, shows his face contorted by hate. There is a fade to a superimposed title in scarlet, "If...."

Notes:

The original screenplay for *If...* was written in 1958 by two under-graduates at Oxford who had been to public (private to Americans) school together. David Sherwin and John Howlett completed the first draft of "Crusaders" by the spring of 1960. Five years later the authors interested

Seth Holt in the project and he took it to Anderson in September of 1966 when he became too involved in his own projects to produce it. Holt took John Howlett to Rome to work with him on another film, which left David Sherwin to complete the script with Anderson. After some scrambling in search of a producer, Paramount Pictures bought the idea. The filming began in March of 1968 with a budget of £250,000. Anderson chose Cheltenham College, his old school, as the setting for the film.

20. O LUCKY MAN! (1973)

Producers:	Michael Medwin, Lindsay Anderson. A SAM (David Sherwin—Lindsay Anderson—Malcolm McDowell) Production.
Director:	Lindsay Anderson
Screenplay:	David Sherwin, based on an original concept by Malcolm McDowell
Photography:	Miroslav Ondricek
Art Direction:	Alan Withy
Set Decorations:	Harry Cordwell
Music Composer and Arranger:	Alan Price
Musicians:	Colin Green (Guitar), Dave Markee (Bass Guitar), Clive Thacker (Drums), Alan Price (Piano).
Songs:	"O Lucky Man!," "Poor People," "Sell Sell," "Look Over Your Shoulder," "Justice," "My Home Town," "Changes."
Songwriter:	Alan Price
Singing:	Alan Price
Sound:	Christian Wangler, Alan Bell, Doug Turner
Wardrobe:	Elsa Fennell
Editors:	Tom Priestley, David Gladwell
Assistant Director:	Derek Cracknell
Make-up:	Paul Rabiger, Basil Newall
Hairdressing:	Colin Jamison
Production Designer:	Jocelyn Herbert
Special Effects:	John Stears
Associate Producer:	Basil Keys
Production Manager:	Don Toms
Cast:	Malcolm McDowell (Mick Travis), Ralph Richardson Monty/Sir James Burgess), Rachel Roberts (Gloria Rowe/Madame Paillard/Mrs. Richards), Arthur Lowe (Mr. Duff/Charlie Johnson/Dr. Munda), Helen Mirren (Patricia Burgess), Dandy Nichols (Tea Lady/Neighbor), Mona Washbourne (Sister Hallett/Usher/Neighbor), Michael Medwin (Army Captain/Power Station Technician/Duke of Belminster), Mary MacLeod (Mrs. Ball/Vicar's Wife/Salvation Army Woman), Vivian Pickles (Welfare Lady), Graham Crowden (Dr. Millar/Professor Stewart/Meths Drinker), Peter Jeffrey (Factory Chairman/Prison Governor), Philip Stone

(Interrogator/Jenkins/Salvation Army Major), Wallas Eaton (Colonel Steiger/John Stone/Warder/Meths Drinker/Film Executive), Anthony Nicholls (General/ Judge/Foreman), Michael Bangerter (Interrogator/ William/Released Prisoner/Assistant), Jeremy Bulloch (Car Crash Victim/Pigboy/Placard Bearer), Warren Clarke (Master of Ceremonies/Male Nurse/Warner), Geoffrey Palmer (Doctor/Basil Keyes), Geoffrey Chater (Vicar/Bishop), Christine Noonan (Coffee Trainee/Girl at Stag Party), Margot Bennett (Coffee Bean Picker), Bill Owen (Superintendent Barlow/ Inspector Carding), Edward Judd (Oswald), Brian Glover (Foreman/Power Station Guard), David Daker, Edward Peel (Policemen), James Bolam (Attenborough/ Doctor), Patricia Healey (Hotel Receptionist), Paul Dawkins (Man at Stag Party/Meths Drinker), Ian Leake (Roadie), Pearl Nunez (Mrs. Naidu), Colin Green (Colin), Clive Thacker (Clive), Dave Markee (Dave), Alan Price (Alan), Lindsay Anderson (Director), Burt Alison, Ben Aris, John Barrett, Sue Bond, Constance Chapman, Peter Childs, Frank Cousins, Brian Coucher, Allen Cullen, Anna Dawson, Kymoke Debayo, Michael Elphick, Eleanor Fazan, Geoff Hinsliff, Jo Jeggo, Patricia Lawrence, Stephenie Lawrence, Brian Lawson, Terence Maidment, Tuesday Miller, Ken Oxtoby, Stuart Perry, Brian Pettifer, Bill Pilkington, Cyril Renison, Irene Richmond, Roy Scammell, Peter Scofield, Frank Singuineau, Patsy Smart, David Stern, Adele Strong, Hugh Thomas, Betty Turner, Glen Williams, Catherine Willmer.

Distribution:	Warner Brothers
Running Time:	166 minutes
Original Running time:	186 minutes

Filmed on location in England and Scotland.

Synopsis

The film opens with a title, "Once Upon a Time . . . ." There is a cut to some peasants working in a field. The film stock is in sepia. The following sequence is silent and punctuated as in the old silent movies by titles. We see a man caught stealing coffee beans from a field; he is taken before a judge by the local police, sentenced, and his hands are cut off. During the sequence the narrative is interrupted by titles such as "Justice," "Unlucky," and "Guilty!" As the camera closes in on the silent scream of the hero when his hands are cut off, the film switches to a title reading "Now." It is immediately followed by a cut to Alan Price and his group of musicians in a recording studio singing the title song, "O Lucky Man!" The credits roll over shots of Price singing the song. The camera swings around the makeshift studio and we get a brief glimpse of Lindsay Anderson in a red shirt supervising the session. The credits and song end together and the film cuts to another title, "West."

The second sequence focuses on Mick Travis, the hero, who is a coffee salesman trainee. We see him being shown around the coffee processing plant, being lectured to by the company public relations woman about the necessity of developing a completely sincere handshake and smile for the customers, and being told that, as Blake once said, anything you believe is so will be so. We learn that the salesman who has been in charge of the northern region has disappeared and Mick has been chosen to take his place. The director of the company outfits him for the job with map, samples, identification card, and pep talk. He is given an apple as he leaves the manager's office. The next scene shows him being seduced by the public relations woman during a coffee tasting session. There is a sudden cut to Alan Price and the musicians again, this time singing a song called "Poor People," in which we are told that someone has to win in the human race and if it isn't you then it has to be me. The film cuts to a long shot of a car traveling through a rather lush countryside. A closer look at the car shows us that it is Mick driving and listening to the radio. Suddenly it is foggy and Mick, who is creeping along, is passed by a red sports car travelling at a high rate of speed. We hear what appears to be a crash, and when Mick comes out of the fog he sees a wreck; the sports car has smashed into a grocery truck. Both the man in the car and the driver of the truck appear to be dead. The police arrive and begin to collect some of the goods scattered on the deserted road. When Mick volunteers to testify about the accident, he is accused by the police of being an obstructionist, and they threaten to arrest him if he doesn't move on. They give him some of the booty and tell him it is "fair dues." He drives off into the fog as they continue to load the trunk of their police car.

The next section is titled "North East" and the car drives into a city; it is night and Mick is listening to a radio program about mental health. He arrives at a hotel, the same one used by his predecessor, and meets the manageress and an old tailor, Bill, who lives in the hotel. They discuss the requirements of the job, youth, ambition, stamina, technical know-how, and luck. During the next Price song, "Sell Sell," we see Mick in a montage of events preparing for his sales pitch. At the end of the song he visits an iron works and learns that they have been closed down and that he has lost one of his biggest customers. A close-up of his sales list shows that he has made a total of 5.97 pounds. He visits a posh hotel and, after a cool reception by the front-desk girl, he meets an oily manager and is told that he will retain the account if he is willing to provide the same arrangements as before. He then accompanies the manager out behind the hotel into the local strip club, where he begins to make "valuable contacts": the chief of police, the local tax man, etc. Mick joins right in the merry-making and gets quite drunk while watching the strip show, the highlight of which is a strip called "chocolate sandwich," which involves two white women and a black man. Arriving back at his hotel he finds the landlady waiting for him in his bed. This interlude is interrupted by an urgent phone call from Gloria, the public relations woman, who tells him to go take over the accounts in Scotland. The phone conversation is abruptly cut off. He packs hurriedly and has another talk with Bill, the tailor, who has made him a gold lamé suit which has magical properties. Bill sends him off with the cryptic remark, "Try not to die like a dog."

The following section begins with the title "North" and we follow Mick
through more countryside as he listens to a variety of religious services on
the radio. He reaches a dead-end road which is blocked by a high fence and,
while peering over it with his binoculars, he is picked up by a group of
soldiers. The radio reports that it will be "a clear day with rain and drizzle at
times." He is taken to an installation which houses an obviously secret
operation. Here he is interrogated and tortured by two civil servants in
business suits who sit and drink tea. They want to know who he is working
for, the Russians, the Germans, the Americans? Suddenly an alarm begins
to ring, and the men leave quickly with Mick still strapped to the torture
chair. A charwoman comes into the room muttering about how messy
people are and unties him. He wanders through the installation which is
now full of smoke and blaring sirens. He escapes with a crowd of people
dressed in white coats. He flees up a hill with the sounds of explosions
following him. Smoke billows behind him and lightning flashes accompany
the noise. He wanders through a desolate landscape of twisted trees and
smoking debris. Suddenly he collapses by a stream, and as he looks up he
sees before him a valley untouched by the fire. As he steps across the stream
to enter the valley, we hear a church bell in the distance. He walks to the
church through the sunshine in his gold lamé suit. The church service is in
progress; it is a harvest festival and the nave is decorated with produce and
flowers. He falls asleep in the back of the church and when he awakens, he
finds himself alone with the vicar's wife and her two children. He is hungry
but she will not let him touch the food. It is God's food, she tells him, and
takes his head in her hands and suckles him at her breast. Afterward, the
children show him the way out of the enchanted valley, and he is told, "there
is nothing for the likes of you in the North." Price's music provides a lyric
interlude as the children bearing flowers and Mick bearing a staff pass
through a pastoral landscape until they come to a highway, where the
children leave him.

He is unexpectedly picked up on the motorway by a Rolls Royce and
whisked off to a private hospital where he is offered money if he will
participate in some medical experiments. He agrees and is run through a
series of tests. On his last night before the "operation," he prowls the
corridors of the clinic and discovers a man's head grafted on the body of a
pig. He flees in terror only to be picked up outside the gates of the
sanitorium by a van full of musicians, Alan Price and his group. They are
heading south and he is comforted by a young "groupie" in the back of the
bus. The title "South" flashes on the screen as the van approaches London in
the early morning. Mick wakes up in the house occupied by the band and the
girl. He joins the girl on the rooftop for a champagne breakfast, where he
confesses his ambition to her. He gestures at a high office building in the
distance and says that he will own something like that someday. She calmly
informs him that her father already does own that one. She describes her
father as "old-fashioned" and "greedy." Mick uses the daughter to gain an
interview with her father, Sir John. While waiting in his outer office, he
witnesses a scene in which one of Sir John's research scientists, distraught
over the work he has done, throws himself out the window, taking Sir
John's private secretary with him. Immediately Mick is hired to replace the

assistant. Sir John and Mick meet with several members of a small foreign country and agree to supply them with "honey," a napalm-like substance, in exchange for the rights to economically exploit the native population. As Alan Price sings "Look Over Your Shoulder" on the soundtrack, Mick becomes the go-between setting up the project. At the last minute, however, he is caught, and Sir John and his associates deny all knowledge of him. He is sent to prison for breaking the law. The courtroom scene in which Mick is convicted is as full of menacing types as was the opening sequence of the film. The judge is flogged by his female clerk in his chambers while the jury is out, and then he publicly condemns Mick for contravening the mores of civilization, telling him that society is based on trust and that he has been greedy. Alan Price sings "Justice."

Mick is released from prison after a talk with the warden, who gives him platitudes and a little book which has been an inspiration to him. He mentions that Mick has eyes like Steve McQueen.

After being given an address of refuge in London by one of the prison guards, the title "East End" flashes on the screen, and we see Mick with his belongings join a group of derelicts at a canteen. He offers to help the woman serving the men and women and is almost killed by a bunch of rummies who hate his patronizing attitude. This episode is followed by another Price interlude during which he sings "Changes." The film cuts to Mick wandering the streets of London. He encounters a man in a sandwich board announcing, "Want to become a Star? Try your Luck." Mick enters a hiring hall where young people are being auditioned for a movie. Lindsay Anderson is sitting at one end of the hall in his red shirt and he spots Mick, motioning for him to come forward. He confronts the young man and asks him to smile. He says, "Why?" and Anderson hits him on the side of the head with a rolled up script, whereupon Mick smiles. The film then abruptly cuts to a cast party in which all the actors who have appeared in the film appear as themselves. This includes Alan Price, who is entertaining the party guests with the verses of "O Lucky Man!" while they dance in a large group.

Notes:

The idea for this film came from Malcolm McDowell. He wrote a script which he called "Coffee Man" based on his personal experiences as a coffee salesman for Chase and Sanborn. He began to write down some of these experiences when he became an actor at Stratford-on-Avon, but it was not until after he had made *If...* and *Figures in a Landscape* that he began to compose them in the form of a script. He had completed it up to the atomic power plant sequence when he met David Sherwin, the script writer for *If....* They decided to collaborate. McDowell told Sherwin the stories and he put them into script form. Over the next year Sherwin, McDowell, and finally Anderson put the script into its final form. Alan Price was brought in to write the music because Anderson had worked with him before on the music for a production of David Storey's "Home," which Anderson staged. Later Anderson wanted to do a documentary on Price but, because of some copyright difficulties, the project was cancelled. Price and Anderson kept in touch with one another and when *O Lucky Man!* got under way, Anderson asked Price to provide a series of Greek chorus interludes for the film. Price actually wrote and performed the music for the film as it was being made rather than for a finished version of the movie. The music was used in a Brechtian sense, not superimposed on the film but integral to it. The original film, which was distributed for public showing in England and for the critics in America, was just a little over three hours in length. The final version, which was shown publicly in the United States, however, was reduced to about two and three-quarter hours in length. The film was cut at the suggestion of Warner Brothers. Three scenes were excised: a Salvation Army segment, a scene where Mrs. Richards commits suicide, and one in which Mick is harassed by a policeman to the song "My Home Town" by Alan Price. The production was headquartered in an abandoned school, St. Paul's Junior School in Hammersmith. The film was made entirely on location: the Kenco Coffee Factory in Wandsworth, a boarding house in Chiswick, the Great Eastern Hotel at Liverpool Street Station, a canteen at the Olympia Exhibition Hall, the Reform Club on Pall Mall, a demolition site at Deptford, and a 13th century church in Kent. The scene of Mick coming out of prison had to be shot in Scotland since security prohibits such on-location shooting in English prisons.

21. IN CELEBRATION (1974)

Producer:	Ely Landau
Production Company:	Ely Landau Organisation (London), Cinevision (Montreal), For The American Film Theater.
Director:	Lindsay Anderson
Screenplay:	David Storey, based on his own play
Photography:	Dick Bush
Art Direction:	Alan Withy
Set Decoration:	Harry Cordwell
Sound Editors:	John Poyner, Stanley Fifeman
Sound Recorder:	Bruce White
Sound Re-recorder:	Dennis Whitlock
Color:	Eastman Color
Editor:	Russell Lloyd
Executive Producer:	Otto Plaschkes
Associate Producer:	Henry T. Weinstein
Production Superintendent:	Jim DiGangi
Production Associate:	Les Landau
Production Manager:	Roy Stevens
Assistant Director:	Richard Jenkins
Additional Music:	Christopher Gunning
Cast:	Alan Bates (Andrew Shaw), James Bolam (Colin Shaw), Brian Cox (Stephen Shaw), Constance Chapman (Mrs. Shaw), Gabrielle Daye (Mrs. Burnett), Bill Owen (Mr. Shaw).

Filmed in Great Britain and Canada.

Distribution: Seven Keys
Running time: 131 minutes

Synopsis

The film opens on a close-up of a turning colliery wheel with piano music in the background. The camera pans to the street below and we see a figure on the sidewalk. The film cuts to the figure meeting a woman on the street at ground level and we follow the young man in through the rear entrance of a row house. We see the interior of the house, a solidly furnished living room with a kitchen at the back. The young man comes in through the back door into the kitchen. He calls out to his father and the elder Shaw comes into the living room from a left doorway. The young man and his father have a rather shy conversation in which the father talks about his age, life in the coal pits, and the uproar the night's festivities have caused with the young man's mother. They discuss the other two sons who are also coming up that afternoon. Mrs. Burnett, a neighbor, drops in and she and Shaw banter back and forth. She asks after Steven's wife and children. They talk about Shaw's developing heart problem and then, with the mention of Colin who has just been promoted at his job, the film cuts away to a young man driving a car and lighting a small cigar. He passes a rather dishevelled man on a roundabout, stops, and backs up. It is the third brother, Andrew. As Colin says to Andrew, "You look like a tramp," and he replies, "I am a tramp," the film cuts back to the sitting room and Steven and Shaw.

The dialogue picks up where it left off before the cut-away. Shaw explains Colin's job to Steven. He is a labor negotiator, and Shaw comments on how ironic the job is, given his working-class family background. Shaw then talks about Andrew, who has just thrown over his job as a lawyer to become an artist. The conversation wanders to references of Shaw's life in the pit until Steven leaves the room to go upstairs to wash up. The film cuts to him upstairs in the lavatory and then out the window to Mrs. Shaw returning. Mrs. Shaw comes into the house below. The couple talk about having tea and Shaw mentions that their son has arrived as Steven enters from the side door. The mother and son exchange pleasantries, with the mother asking after Steven's wife and children. They also discuss Shaw's coming out of the pit. Shaw talks about the value of education and of his wife's degree in domestic science, and the fact that her father was a pig breeder (a freeholder, she corrects).

The film cuts to an exterior aerial shot of the coal town and we see Colin's car coming down one of the streets. A close-up of the car follows as Andrew breezes out and into the front door of the house. Colin drives away saying that there isn't a safe place to park in the neighborhood. Andrew arrives in the living room and surprises Mrs. Shaw. He teases her and makes jokes about the room looking like a museum, not having changed in 5,000 years. Andrew keeps up a barrage of this sort of banter, both teasing and goading his mother. He talks about his art, "You think I'm painting young ladies with no clothes on." He says that he does abstract paintings. Andrew maintains this steady flow of dialogue, touching on his father's taste in reading (westerns), and his mother's mania for cleanliness. There is a quick cut-away to a shot of Colin trudging up the street carrying two bags. Mrs. Shaw goes to the rear of the house to look for Colin, who comes in the side door. Andrew remarks about Colin coming in the front door like royalty. Colin seems a little bewildered by Andrew's banter. The scene is resolved with the entrance of Steven and Shaw who have been at a pub.

The whole family now kids one another. The conversation is interrupted by a cut to Colin and his mother in the kitchen. She is fixing tea. After the tea is served, the conversation turns to Steven's projected work. He admits that he has all but abandoned it. It was a work on modern society and how man has succumbed to a passivity in modern life. Mrs. Burnett arrives and joins the Shaws for tea. Andrew twits her about the family setting up a glass coffin business. The conversation evolves to memories of the boys when they were children, the Shaws' marriage, and finally the death of Jamey, another of the Shaws' children. Both Shaw and his wife exit to get ready for the anniversary party the boys are giving them at one of the posh local hotels. The three boys are left alone in the living room downstairs.

Colin cautions Andrew about his goading both of himself and his parents. The three boys reminisce about how poor they were while they were growing up. Colin admits his fear of being poor again and the social humiliation he suffered in school because of it. Andrew razzes Colin about his job. The boys confess their guilt about the death of Jamey, each revealing the scars he bears because of the event. They also discuss how the death affected their parents: the father's despondency and the mother's withdrawal from the eldest, Andrew. Steven has been having nightmares about Jamey. The boys admit to their over-education. They have been educated out of their class and away from their roots. The confessions are interrupted by Shaw's entrance. He is obviously not used to being dressed up. He cautions the boys to admire their mother's outfit when she comes in, which they all do. They all troop out of the room accompanied by their family banter. Steven remains behind and for a moment looks around the room until he is summoned by his mother from off camera. This scene ends the first act of the film.

The second act begins with the camera opening up on Mrs. Burnett. She has come in to bank the fire for the Shaws, and now stands reading a postcard on the mantle. Andrew sneaks in behind her and tickles her. Everyone files into the living room, talking about how wonderful the evening was. Shaw breaks out some whiskey and persuades Mrs. Burnett to stay and have a glass. They talk about how grand the restaurant was and about how Colin bought some champagne. Shaw mentions all of the mill owners and city bigwigs he saw at the restaurant. The family toasts the couple and Mrs. Burnett. The conversation shifts to Shaw's life in the coal pits. He admits that no one can know just how bad it really is unless they have been down into the pits just once. The conversation moves from the pits to a shelter they all occupied during the war and of the happy hours they spent playing cards by candlelight. Mrs. Shaw begins to hum a hymn tune and soon everyone except Steven is singing. The talk turns to Sunday School and the boys' recollections of it, which brings up Jamey again. Shaw admits his grief, at the close of which Mrs. Shaw announces that she needs to go to bed. With her exit Mrs. Burnett goes as well. The boys discuss where they will all sleep, and Shaw retires with a remark about the value of the family.

The following scenes are full of tension and potential violence as the three boys, now alone, begin to reveal the true feelings which lie under the polite facade they have been maintaining all evening. Andrew is once again the goad as he forces the other two to expose their feelings. Andrew disappears upstairs and the camera follows him. He sees Steven crying and returns downstairs. He wakes up Colin to talk. Shaw comes in, having also been awakened by Steven's crying. Andrew goes upstairs to waken Steven and returns announcing that he was only bothered by a dream. Steven comes in and interrupts his monologue. Andrew goes to the food at the hotel as an explanation for Steven's dream. Andrew then begins on his mother after Shaw cautions him about waking her. The other boys try to excuse Andrew's tirade, claiming that he is drunk. Colin becomes more and more disturbed by his brother's dissection of the family relationships. Steven begins to cry and Shaw cries with him. Andrew continues. He points out the fruitless sacrifices the boys have made to education and to the pointless sacrifice Shaw has made down in the pits to atone for the loss of Jamey, who was the cause of the marriage in the first place, since Mrs. Shaw was pregnant before they wed. The scene concludes with Steven's remark that Shaw's work has significance for him in a way that the jobs his sons have do not. The fury over, the boys part and go to bed.

Scene two of the second act opens with Mrs. Shaw coming in to the living room, ready to make breakfast. It is now morning and she wakes up Colin, who has been sleeping in the chair. This last scene has the same surface politeness that the opening did. Mrs. Shaw begins to talk about the time after Jamey died when they sent Andrew away for a while. She does not pursue this, though, and calls Shaw to come down for breakfast. Colin admits to his mother that he may be getting married soon, a confession he had made to his brothers the night before. She is pleased and remarks that she knew something was up by his mood. She tells Shaw the news when he comes in but he barely reacts. She tells Andrew when he comes in and he reacts mockingly. Andrew once again assumes the role of catalyst. He announces to Steven that Colin is getting married. Steven is politely responsive. The boys make plans for leaving. Colin helps his mother clean up the largely uneaten breakfast. Andrew throws out several remarks which suggest the tensions of the night before. The boys stiffen but Mrs. Shaw remains unaware of the import of the allusions. Andrew starts in on his mother.

She misses or pretends to miss the point of what he is saying. Finally, she remarks about what a funny family they have. Mrs. Burnett arrives to say good-bye to the boys. They go through a series of conventional farewells with the parents except that after Steven has taken his father's hand, he embraces him. Shaw and Mrs. Burnett follow the boys outside as the camera cuts to an exterior of the house with Colin's car in front. Mrs. Shaw appears at the window and looks out at the departing sons. Shaw comes to the curb to see them off. The camera cuts to an overhead shot of the car driving off and then cuts to the revolving colliery wheel and the piano music. This shot holds as the credits roll.

Notes:

This film was made for the highly acclaimed American Film Theater following Anderson's successful production of the play in London. It is one of several plays by David Storey that he has directed. He used the original cast of the London performance with the exception of Fulton MacKay who played Reardon, a character who was cut entirely from the film version of the drama. The play is substantially the same as the published version with some minor cuts, some rearranging of dialogue, and the exclusion of Reardon.

NOTES

1. Anderson's first four films, *Meet the Pioneers, Idlers that Work, Three Installations,* and *Wakefield Express,* are not available for viewing in the United States. The synopses of these films are based on information supplied in Elizabeth Sussex, *Lindsay Anderson* (New York: Frederick A. Praeger, 1969).
2. *Trunk Conveyor,* the trailers for the National Society for the Prevention of Cruelty to Children—*Green and Pleasant Land, Henry, The Children Upstairs,* and *A Hundred Thousand Children,* and the shorts for the National Industrial Fuel Efficiency Service £20 a Ton and *Energy First* are also not available for viewing in this country. The information on *Trunk Conveyor* is available in Elizabeth Sussex, *Lindsay Anderson.* The NSPCC supplied me with résumés of their films. Lindsay Anderson supplied me with the information about £20 a Ton. He could not remember anything about *Energy First.*
3. *The White Bus* is not distributed in the United States. The information for the synopsis of this film was gleaned from a number of sources: Elizabeth Sussex, *Lindsay Anderson,* and the film reviews (*see* no. 94, 97, 99).

Annotated Guide to Writings

1949

22. Grierson, John and Phillip Mackie. "Welcome Stranger!" *Sight and Sound,* 18 (Spring), 51.

A brief notice highlighting the British film journal *Sequence,* of which Anderson was one of the editors. The authors see it as "brave, irreverent and new." Grierson thought it heralded a new generation of film critics and gave it his blessing. The journal is summed up as "new and fresh and lively. Set it against the commonplace enthusiasms and routine facetiousness of most current film criticism, and it looks like the Boy Wonder making rings around a punch-drunk old pug."

1952

23. Hauser, Frank. Review of *Making a Film. Sight and Sound,* 22 (June), 182.

A generally complimentary review of Anderson's book *Making a Film: The Story of "Secret People"* (see no. 381). The reviewer suggests, however, that the reader might be inclined to ask questions about some of the film's weaknesses and virtues. Since the book is about the making of a single film, rather than about filmmaking in general, there is little guidance given to the reader to assist him in making value judgments. The reviewer finds Anderson's style "clean, likeable English," and an enhancement to the book's usefulness.

1953

24. Anon. "The Pleasure Garden." *Sight and Sound,* 22 (January-March), 114.

This photo-essay about the making of James Broughton's film *The Pleasure Garden* in the gardens of the Crystal Palace mentions that Anderson was in charge of production and played a small part.

1954

25. Barnes, Peter. Review of *Thursday's Children. Films and Filming,* 1, no. 3 (December), 20.

Describes the documentary film as: "Simple and unpretentious in style, the film's deep compassion never slides into sentimentality." "The directors have focused their attention solely on these unaffected and completely unselfconscious deaf children, and the film glows with their innocence and goodness." Obviously a labor of love, the film is remarkably successful in capturing the spirit of the children and their lives.

26. Kael, Pauline. *I Lost It at the Movies.* Boston: Little, Brown and Company, pp. 15-18, 63, 99-100.

Kael pans *This Sporting Life* as a film which "makes a simple, though psychologically confused, story look complex, and modern because inexplicable." She has little patience with viewers who find fast editing and out-of-normal sequences more "cinematic" than the usual storytelling, because they make it difficult for the audience to follow the action. She concludes by paraphrasing Anderson about the tragedy of the story and its uniqueness: "A tragedy without a story is unique all right: a disaster." There are also references to Free Cinema and *Every Day Except Christmas.*

1955

27. Bardon, D. Letter to the Editor. *Sight and Sound,* 24 (Spring), 216.

The author of this letter is a psychiatrist who questions Anderson's conclusions in his analysis of *On the Waterfront* (*see* no. 403), even though Bardon did find the essay stimulating. The rest of the letter deals with Bardon's criticism of Anderson's conclusions: he disagrees with the Christian interpretation of Terry Malloy's final walk to the shed, and he argues with Anderson that the final crowd scene is a good example of unionism.

28. De La Roche, Catherine. Letter to the Editor. *Sight and Sound,* 24 (Spring), 216.

With lucidity and conviction, De La Roche writes very strongly in favor of Anderson's article about *On the Waterfront* (*see* no. 403), and the moral implications of the film. She congratulates *Sight and Sound* for giving Anderson the space to develop his argument adequately.

29. Glover, Guy. Letter to the Editor. *Sight and Sound,* 24 (Spring), 218-219.

Glover uses a letter to the editor of *Sight and Sound* by Anderson (*see* no. 394) criticizing John Grierson to argue with the magazine's handling of the short film. He feels that they have been inadequately covered and as a Canadian, he also feels that more Canadian films should be reviewed.

30. Jones, G. H. Letter to the Editor. *Sight and Sound,* 24 (Spring), 216.

The author of this letter agrees with some of Anderson's conclusions about *On the Waterfront* (*see* no. 403), but wonders why he applies an analysis of the symbolic nature of the last portion of the film to the entirety. He sees this as a growing and alarming tendency of much of the recent *Sight and Sound* criticism, i.e. to disparage directors of "great technical ability" who sometimes produce "pretentious, hollow monuments to their skill as technicians" by applying moral standards along the lines which Anderson suggests.

31. Kleiner, B. Letter to the Editor. *Sight and Sound,* 24 (Spring), 216.

Praises Anderson's article about *On the Waterfront* (*see* no. 403), and especially his comparison of *The Grapes of Wrath* with *Pinky.* The author used to refer to Kazan's work as "Socialromantik" or "Soci-romanticism."

32. Lambert, Gavin. Review of *Thursday's Children. Sight and Sound*, 25, no. 1 (Summer), 36.

Praises the film as midway between a documentary and a personal impression. It is, however, "the freshest, most human short film to be made in this country since *David*." He also praises Anderson and Guy Brenton for their "unusual purity of emotional response" in capturing the world of the deaf and dumb children in a most accuate and sensitive way.

33. Spencer, Charles S. Letter to the Editor. *Sight and Sound*, 24 (Spring), 216.

Spencer finds Anderson's criticisms in the *On the Waterfront* article (*see* no. 403) not only subjective but almost dishonest. He feels that Anderson saw the film, disliked it, and is now fabricating an intellectual argument as a basis for his reaction.

34. Urb, Len. Letter to the Editor. *Sight and Sound*, 24 (Spring), 216.

The author praises Anderson for his excellent essay about *On the Waterfront* (*see* no. 403). He agrees that the main point of the film is that collective action on the part of the union members is insufficient to clean up the union, and that only the individual heroics of Terry Malloy are effective.

1956

35. Anon. "The Front Page." *Sight and Sound*, 26 (Winter), 115.

A brief notice about the press comment on Anderson's article "Stand Up! Stand Up!" (*see* no. 414) which had been considerable. The press categorizes the Left as responding to the article by underlining the political implications, and the Center and Right as characterizing it as an "artificial exercise" for testing the reactions of others. The editors of *Sight and Sound* support Anderson's main point, which is that cinema is a social force as well as an art form, and many films have "more to say about our society than the uncommitted critic may admit." In response to the challenge of one of their readers, *Sight and Sound* was going to run a survey of British documentary in the Spring issue.

36. Astor, David. Letter to the Editor. *Sight and Sound*, 26 (Winter), 163.

The writer is angered by Anderson's article "Stand Up! Stand Up!" (*see* no. 414) which criticized an exhibition mounted by *The Observer* called "Sixty Years of Cinema." He finds it odd that Anderson's article should have appeared in *Sight and Sound*, which is published from the offices of the British Film Institute, the organization which chose the stills for *The Observer* exhibition.

37. Baillie, M. I. Letter to the Editor. *Sight and Sound*, 26 (Winter), 163-164.

Baillie agrees with Anderson in "Stand Up! Stand Up!" (*see* no. 414) that a critic should have a point of view and that films should be judged from an aesthetic standpoint but not from a "non-partisan" viewpoint.

38. Denton, Clive. Letter to the Editor. *Sight and Sound*, 26 (Winter), 164.

He feels that "Stand Up! Stand Up!" (*see* no. 414) was both "timely and welcome, and yet sad," sad because he feels that it is unnecessary for *Sight and Sound* to trumpet the tune it has played for years, "that films must be personal and pregnant, that style, beyond proficiency, is no more than useful, that the people who make films are less important than the people films are about."

39. Kapp, Helen. Letter to the Editor. *Sight and Sound,* 26 (Winter), 163.
    "As a painter and director of an Art Gallery and Museum, I am concerned with exactly the same problems that Mr. Anderson discusses in his article, 'Stand Up! Stand Up!' " (*see* no. 414). She is disturbed by the "non-committed" critic who creates confusion rather than enlightenment. She agrees with Anderson that critics should uphold standards rather than pretending that they do not exist.

40. Lambert, Gavin. "Free Cinema." *Sight and Sound,* 25 (Spring), 173-177.
    Reviews the first of the Free Cinema shows at the National Film Theatre and discusses the humanism and point of view which ties these otherwise disparate films together. *O Dreamland* is one of these movies and Lambert provides a rather detailed analysis of the film. The *papier maché* facade and unrelieved ugliness of the amusement park are photographed in stark realism, but the humanism of the director comes through to moderate our reactions to the people who listlessly take their pleasure by the seaside. "The pleasures are sad not because they are ugly but because there is nothing else."

41. Lambert, Gavin. Letter to the Editor. *Sight and Sound,* 26 (Winter), 164-165.
    Makes several references to Anderson and his films (*O Dreamland, Thursday's Children*), and to "Stand Up! Stand Up!" (*see* no. 414) which he felt was a fine article. Lambert agrees wholeheartedly with Anderson that criticism does not exist in a vacuum and must be given a social context.

42. Manvell, Roger. Letter to the Editor. *Sight and Sound,* 26 (Winter), 163.
    Praises Anderson who, in his article "Stand Up! Stand Up!" (*see* no. 414) points out the "dry rot" which has overtaken much of the writing about films. Manvell feels that "Stand Up! Stand Up!" is the most important statement of principle ever published in *Sight and Sound.* He heartily agrees with Anderson that "art (and film as art) can only possess real artistic values if the human, social values expressed are themselves enlightened."

43. Stringer, Michael. Letter to the Editor. *Sight and Sound,* 26 (Winter), 163.
    Praises Anderson's call for a "committed" film criticism in "Stand Up! Stand Up!" (*see* no. 414). The author feels that the reason for so much of the pessimism in contemporary writing about film is that it is uncommitted.

44. Taylor, J. R. Letter to the Editor. *Sight and Sound,* 26 (Winter), 164.
    Asks whether Anderson, in his article "Stand Up! Stand Up!" (*see* no. 414) is offering his readers any guide on to what one should be committed. Taylor admits that critics should be engaged and have a point of view, but "committed to what?" he asks. Finally, he feels that Anderson is doing little more than presenting us with a "short guide to his personal prejudices."

1957

45. Berger, John. "Look at Britain!" *Sight and Sound,* 27 no. 1 (Summer), 12-14.

Discusses Anderson's *Every Day Except Christmas* as an affectionate film about the Covent Garden workers. The film derives its special quality from the fact that Anderson approaches his subject on a basis of equality, which puts his characters at ease and eliminates any self-consciousness in front of the camera. Anderson's single-mindedness and the superb rhythm of the film create its impact. Berger is critical of the lack of economic determinism in the film, which would have been the stuff of the documentary in the Thirties. Nevertheless, Anderson's images are compounded into a powerful film.

46. Houston, Penelope. "Captive or Free." *Sight and Sound,* 27 (Winter), 116-120.

This review of the "Captive Cinema" program at the National Film Theatre contrasts it with the Free Cinema programs of the two previous years. The main difference between the two schools of documentary seems to be one of approach. The Captive Cinema people want to capture the fact, people being who they are. The Free Cinema directors, represented best by Anderson, want to shape the facts in order to present a particular idea to the audience. The first writes in terms of fact; Anderson, in terms of "conviction."

47. Jackson, Frank. Letter to the Editor. *Sight and Sound,* 26 (Spring), 220-221.

Jackson agrees with Anderson's criticism of contemporary film journalism in "Stand Up! Stand Up!" (*see* no. 414). He is a writer for a "popular Sunday newspaper" and feels that the journalists, by giving the people what they think they want, are helping to foster the deterioration of popular taste, to which Anderson calls attention. Jackson's suggestion, however, is that rather than attacking the journalists, the public should become more active readers and critics of the daily press and demand higher standards.

48. O'Brien, Richard. Letter to the Editor. *Sight and Sound,* 26(Spring), 220.

Anderson's article "Stand Up! Stand Up!" (*see* no. 414) prompted this writer to ask why so few films are made which deal actively with industrial problems—is it because they would be too violent and too full of conflict?

49. Robinson, David. "Looking for Documentary, Part Two: The Ones That Got Away." *Sight and Sound,* 27 (Autumn), 70-75.

Describes Anderson as "one of the most articulate and individual artists working in the British cinema today." His reputation, however, was based on documentary films alone, and a body of "highly personal, shrewd and vigorous criticism." He mentions the theme of men and their relationship to work which pervades the early films like *Wakefield Express, Foot and Mouth* and *Every Day Except Christmas.* Robinson also mentions the trailers made for the NSPCC (*Green and Pleasant Land, Henry* and *The Children Upstairs*), which recall Franju's *Le Sang des Bêtes.* Anderson's films characterize the best of the Free Cinema movement.

1958

50. Houston, Penelope. Review of *March to Aldermaston. Sight and Sound,* 28 no. 2 (Spring), 89.

Mentions that the film was made by a team of "anonymous technicians" although the publicity sheet mentions a committee of 11. She sees a conflict between the TV people and film people in the creation of the film; the balance is never quite achieved.

51. Jacobs, Lewis. "New Trends in British Documentary: Free Cinema." *Film Culture*, no. 17 (February), 8-10.

A brief analysis of both *O Dreamland* and *Every Day Except Christmas*, treating them as films which deal with people as individuals, rather than with issues, the latter being a traditional concern of British documentaries. *O Dreamland* is described as "a sardonic comment upon popular culture," contrasting "the nightmare world of tawdry distractions at an amusement park with the apathetic search of its motley group of pleasure-seekers," *Every Day Except Christmas* as "a portfolio of honest, direct, unsubtle and sometimes strong portraits of the night workers at Covent Garden market."

1959

52. Burch, Noel. "Four French Documentaries." *Film Quarterly*, 13, no. 1 (Fall), 56-61.

Fleeting mention of Anderson's ability for using film technique to "get at the heart" of the subject in contrast to the French filmmakers who use the material as the basis for a personal fantasy.

53. McCarthy, Matt. "Free Cinema in Chains." *Films and Filming*, 5 (February), 10, 17.

The author calls into question the impact of the Free Cinema movement. As he sees it, the movement has had practically no effect on the world of the commercial film. He does not see how the films from the movement could have fulfilled what he describes as the filmmaker's "middle-class socialist" expectations, and denies that the films can even awaken any "humanist enthusiasm" in the audience.

1960

54. Kitchin, Laurence. "Lindsay Anderson," in *Mid-Century Drama*. London: Faber & Faber, pp. 193-195.

Praises Anderson's move to the theater from the mass media. It also corrects somewhat the statement Anderson made in the *Declaration* article (*see* no. 421) about "unrealistic liberal aspiration" which he would now modify. He still feels that the social position in Britain does provide a "wonderful opportunity and challenge to artists."

55. Mekas, Jonas. "Cinema of the New Generation." *Film Culture*, 21 (Summer), 1-6.

Mentions Anderson's *O Dreamland* and *Every Day Except Christmas* as two of the independently made films which inaugurated the Free Cinema movement at the National Film Theatre in the spring of 1956.

56. Storey, David. *This Sporting Life*. New York: Macmillan.

The novel for Anderson's film.

1961

57. Anon. "Free Cinema and Where It Was Leading To." *Filmkritik*, no. 3, pp. 140-49.

This account in German of the Free Cinema movement stresses the connections between the documentaries and the current fiction films coming out of England. The author also mentions the beginnings of the movement in the pages of *Sequence.*

58.   Anon. "Production in Britain." *Sight and Sound,* 30 (Summer), 122.
Mentions that Anderson was beginning work on *This Sporting Life;* the casting was not yet complete.

1962

59.   Anon. "Qu-est-ce que le Free Cinema?" *Positif,* (December), pp. 13-14.
This French account of the Free Cinema movement stresses the relationship between the politics of *Sequence,* where the original tenets of the movement were set forth, and the final working out of those ideas in the British Film Institute programs. Places the objectives of the film program parallel to the philosophic revolt of the "Angry Young Men."

60.   Milne, Tom. *"This Sporting Life." Sight and Sound,* 31, no. 3 (Summer), 122.
Milne sees Anderson as the one of all "the directors in, round, behind, or stemming from the Free Cinema movement, [who] has by far the most recognizable, most personal style." In a country in which the theater has developed into a "healthy and provocative movement," Anderson has taken some remarkable strides toward freeing the cinema from the apron strings of the novel and the play, "to be free to invent a bit of film instead of filming a bit of script." He feels that *This Sporting Life* does this by becoming Anderson's film rather than Storey's novel. Instead of focusing on the north country environment, social climbing, or any other of the usual trappings left over from *Room at the Top,* Anderson emphasizes the tragedy of a man "who achieves his ambition for fame" but then, helpless, steers himself and the woman he loves to disaster. The quality he achieves is close to Antonioni. The film is more formalized than is usual for the *nouvelle vague* approach and more stylish than a rough-hewn or thrown-together look often used to convey the "impressions of raw life." "Anderson readily agrees that a signature is essential, that film is, or should be, a language."

1963

61.   Alpert, Hollis. "The Real Life." *Saturday Review,* 46 (13 July), 16
Alpert begins his review with: "How is it, for instance, that the British manage so frequently to come up with films that combine good drama with uncompromising views of contemporary life?" He sees Anderson's *This Sporting Life* as fitting into and transcending that tradition. Despite a few moments of strained credulity, the film in general receives firm treatment. Everything rings true; the atmosphere of the rugger games, the locker rooms, the pubs, even the dance hall seem "sharp and authentic."

62.   Anon. Review of *This Sporting Life. Filmfacts,* 6 (25 July), 139-141.
Contains a detailed list of the film's credits, a synopsis, and a sampling of the reviews, most of them positive. The one exception is the *Time* magazine piece. Among the critiques excerpted are: Judith Crist, *New York Herald Tribune* (*see* no.

68); A. H. Weiler, the *New York Times* (*see* no. 82); Stanley Kaufmann, *The New Republic* (*see* no. 75); Hollis Alpert, *The Saturday Review* (*see* no. 61); and Jay Cocks, *Time* (*see* no. 66).

63. Anon. Review of *This Sporting Life*. *Manchester Guardian* (6 February), p. 6.

This film, in spite of its "new-wave pretentiousness," is cliché-ridden in both script and direction. The Rugby League background is unconvincing, the flashbacks hackneyed, and the relationship between Machin and the widow unconvincing. Still there are many signs of talent in the film.

64. Anon. Review of *This Sporting Life*. *The New York Times Magazine* (14 April), pp. 126-127.

A picture essay with a number of stills from the film, noting that Richard Harris, then starring in *Mutiny on the Bounty*, "may make a greater impact on the public as the athlete." Anderson will be a director to watch.

65. Baker, Peter. Review of *This Sporting Life*. *Films and Filming*, 9, no. 6 (March), 32.

"If I have over-praised *This Sporting Life*, it is because I was expecting arrogance and saw compassion, expected Socialism and saw an apolitical humanity. It is a film to delight anyone who enjoys craftsmanship in the cinema; it is a film to make you think; and, I hope for a great mass audience, it is a film in the best sense, to entertain." Baker goes on to compare the style with the complications of *Citizen Kane*, and to praise Anderson for his recognition "that art of its very nature owes some allegiance to tradition." He does criticize Anderson for handling actors in a way which betrays his "long stint at the Royal Court"; the scenes sometimes smack of stage acting, and Anderson has a tendency to pose his characters for "big" moments instead of allowing the bigness to spring from the action itself. It is finally the structure which delights the critic the most: "There is never any sense of gimmickry or intellectual snobbism; instead, a sense of honest craftsmanship applied to the problem of how to best project the story."

66. Cocks, Jay. "Slummox." *Time*, 82 (19 July), 78.

"In the past five years the Angry Generation of British moviemakers has whacked off several vivid slices of working-class life.... Sooner or later it was bound to cut off a hunk of baloney, and this is it." Jay Cocks did not like the story of a man with a "huge body and a tiny soul." He says the story makes more sense on paper than on film, and that the plot splinters into flashbacks which the audience must spend half its time putting together. The whole picture finally seems unreasonable and unmotivated.

67. Coleman, John. "Another Kind of Loving." *New Statesman*, 65 (15 February), 246.

Praises Anderson's handling of the characters in *This Sporting Life* as an extremely professional job and concedes that he is an important accession to the "thin ranks" of British directors. Anderson's elevation of Machin into *the hero*, however, is awkwardly treated.

68. Crist, Judith. "'This Sporting Life' Glows." *New York Herald Tribune* (17 July), p. 10.

The film is a "brilliantly ruthless portrait of a professional football player and his brutish world." The plot is secondary since the film is about one man's self-examination. Crist is impressed by the skillful weaving of the impressionistic photography and the realistic soundtrack in this first feature film of Anderson's.

69. D., P. J. Review of *This Sporting Life*. *Monthly Film Bulletin*, 30, no. 350 (March), 34.

Finds that British filmmaking needed a film as "uncommonly whole-hearted" as *This Sporting Life*. The love affair between the central characters is "profound"; Anderson's visual sense is remarkably strong; and finally there is "an hypnotic, almost mid-European abstractness about several of the later scenes." The film provides "an opportunity for deep personal expression," a quality one cannot help but realize and return "with a similarly full and grateful response."

70. Delaney, Shelagh. "The White Bus," in *Sweetly Sings the Donkey*. New York: G. P. Putnam's Sons, pp. 165-186.

The short story which is the basis of Anderson's film.

71. Gilliatt, Penelope. "A Great Week for British Cinema." *The Observer Weekend Review* (10 February), p. 20.

This Sporting Life is described as having a "blow like a fist." The reviewer had never seen a British picture which "gave such expression to the violence and the capacity for pain that there is in the English character." She finds the film hard to write about because all the important elements are sub-verbal: the power, the pain, and the anger.

72. Hartung, Philip T. Review of *This Sporting Life*. *Commonweal*, 78 (9 August), 480.

Although the film is a bit too violent for his tastes, especially the scene where Machin gets his teeth knocked out, the critic feels the film exhibits originality and artistry. He particularly admires the filmmaking, not only by Anderson, but also the fine production by Karel Reisz, and David Storey's good, uncompromising script. Plot is not the main thing in the film: "Characterization is foremost, and the film is crowded with well-played small roles that add to its richness." The author is also fascinated by Anderson's technique in the skillfully directed rugby and locker room scenes, and with the flashbacks which keep the audience "on their toes" by requiring them to "think and work" with the director. It is a "thoughtful film, one that will stay with you a long time."

73. Houston, Penelope. *The Contemporary Cinema*. Baltimore, Md.: Penguin Books, pp. 113-114 and passim.

Anderson is discussed in the context of the importance of the "Free Cinema" movement both in the history of British cinema and in its influence throughout the world cinema. Houston recalls the importance of the "everyday" in the documentaries which came out of that movement. Anderson wanted to make ordinary people feel their dignity and importance. These ideas spilled over into the commercial films made later by the "Free Cinema" directors.

74. Howard, Ivor. Review of *This Sporting Life*. *Films in Review*, 14, no. 7 (August-September), 437-438.

"Lindsay Anderson's direction couldn't have been clumsier, especially in the opening sequences, in which he breaks off the action to interpolate stream-of-consciousness flashbacks in order to indicate the past of his oafish non-hero." The author sees this film as reflecting the "so-called 'committed' (politically) filmmakers of Britain" whose "portrayals of life are about as realistic as their lavender-leftism, and about as socially stultifying." The poor script, the poor acting, along with the poor direction make the film dreary indeed.

75. Kauffman, Stanley. "The Footballer and the Lady." *New Republic,* 149 (20 June), 25-26.

Kauffman praises Anderson's ability to make the film "respond to life with immediacy and heat," especially in the rugby scenes, "all brawn and smash." He also likes Anderson's adroitly interwoven flashback sequences and the excellent performances turned in by Richard Harris and Rachel Roberts. The basic fault in the film lies in the thematic flaw in the script which separates the football story from the love story. Several other objections he has focus on the film's wavering viewpoint, the failure of the whole last sequence, a "disintegration, not a conclusion," and the inconsistent secondary characters.

76. LaBadie, Donald W. Review of *This Sporting Life. Show,* 3 (August), 24-25.

The critic notes that Anderson's focus on the characters as individuals and not class representatives moves the film out of the category of working-class epic. This "outstanding feature film debut" launches Anderson as a stylist of individual talent who sidesteps the clichés which are already honeycombing the new cinema.

77. Millar, Gavin. "Against *This Sporting Life*." *Movie,* no. 10, pp. 21-22.

This review begins, "One feels guilty about attacking *This Sporting Life* because of the ambitiousness of its intentions." He goes on, "One can only admire this unprecedented—in Britain—attempt to portray a complex relationship with passion instead of gutless understatement." In fact Millar admits there would be no need to attack the movie at all except that its critical acceptance threatened to make it an instant classic film of the "resurrected British cinema." It is Anderson's fragmentary technique which bothers Millar the most, largely because the omnipresent use of the close-up forces the audience to identify and find praiseworthy the main character, Frank Machin, a position that the critic does not approve. Not only does he object to overpraising the film, especially from *Sight and Sound,* but he also finds the film irritating to watch. He dislikes the "search for impact in the use of sound track, camera angles and shock cutting," and the "expressionistic" devices in the film are disastrous. Finally, he sums up Anderson's style by describing it as failing to be oppressive by becoming repressive, and as a result we lose our moral awareness of Frank Machin which stunts the moral growth of the film.

78. Oliver, Edith. "Smashing Away." *The New Yorker,* 39 (20 July), 72.

Feels that when the picture is over the audience has been as much "pummelled and shaken by the noise and vehemence as by the tragedy of poor Machin." Anderson "seems to treat his principal character, in one sudden closeup after another, as a zoological specimen rather than a man." Although she likes the film, she feels that, like *Saturday Night and Sunday Morning,* it is "terribly over-directed, with an often purposeless insistence on brash, though skillful, shots of the particulars of working-class life."

79. St. Pierre, Brian. "*This Sporting Life*: Bigger Than Life." *Seventh Art,* 1, no. 4 (Fall), 13, 28-29.

Describes *This Sporting Life* as "the most exciting directorial debut since Truffaut's." He sees Anderson as having lifted "British cinema from its grim and grimy prison," and he regards the last seven years of British cinema as a prelude to this film. The author praises the visceral qualities of the film,"all guts and emotion, real and raw, hitting you in the belly and making you ache." He also singles out Anderson's direction which is assured, the sharp cutting, and the brilliantly timed use of sound overlaps, which far surpasses Tony Richardson's use of the same technique in *The Loneliness of a Long Distance Runner*. He is equally impressed by Anderson's handling of actors, a quality he attributes to his stage experience. Finally, he is most impressed with the way Anderson shaped the script with the camera, "patting here, tramping it down there, pushing and pulling it into shape," and in the process he stamps it with his personality.

80. Silke, James. Review of *This Sporting Life*. *Cinema*, 1, no. 6 (November-December), 44.

Praises the creation of the Machin character by Richard Harris and denies that he is "pathetic, a victim of society, a miserable animal." Instead, largely as a result of the incisive cutting of Anderson, "cutting as sharp and painful as an elbow to the gut," Harris has created "a yelling, spitting, bleeding male animal," one who does not draw pity but admiration for not being ground down by the tragedy of his life. Anderson's first directorial task is "a blinder, as they say in rugby matches . . . sheer guts, imagination and heart."

81. Walsh, Moira. Review of *This Sporting Life*. *America*, 109 (31 August), 219.

Anderson's *This Sporting Life* is not a successful whole; it "obviously intends to say more than it manages to convey." Also critical of Anderson's choice of material; "human degradation and human failure" are valid subjects for the cinema, she says, but she finds them indicative of the film as a whole: "The dimensions of a well-ordered human life are not detectable at all in this British film." Also rather critical of what she calls Anderson's "rather arty experimentation with stream-of-consciousness flashbacks."

82. Weiler, A. H. "Screen: 'This Sporting Life' Arrives." *The New York Times* (17 July), p. 19.

Sees the film as a smashing success for a first effort on the part of the Anderson-Harris-Reisz team. The complicated stream-of-consciousness approach gives way to lucid, realistic stuff "as tough and genuine as the rough rugby star on whom it is centered."

83. Vas, Robert. "Arrival and Departure." *Sight and Sound*, 32, no. 2 (Spring), 56-59.

This film provides a happy discovery, a discovery that in Britain there seems to be "an audience, producers, actors and writers for this new Realism." Lindsay Anderson has freed himself from his past and the "direct attack, the deliberate harnessing of poetry to propaganda," in order to throw himself, courageously and "with such hungry intensity into the complicated texture, interaction and social background of human feelings." Vas finds the interaction between the flashbacks and the present, the subjective point of view, even the shifts for objective clarification, contributing to the creation and development of the central character, Frank Machin. He does not think that the love story between landlady and footballer is in conflict with the focus on Machin's career as a rugger player;

rather, he sees the emphasis on Machin's career as providing background material for the later focus of the film on the romance. While acknowledging those scenes which the other critics have hauled out for punishment, Vas prefers to concentrate on those which do work well within the context of the film. He singles out the idyllic scene with Machin and the children playing in the country, the moments of Machin's frustration when he resorts to physical violence, and the "visionary" rugby scene with which the film closes. He concludes: "But it is an arrival as much as a departure; a breakthrough perhaps to a more demanding audience, and more courage in production; a password to the unashamed expression of emotion."

1964

84. Anon. Review of *This Sporting Life. International Film Guide*, 1: 76.

Anderson has fulfilled the promise of his "vitriolic criticism" in *O Dreamland* and *Every Day Except Christmas* by fashioning an "unhandsome story" out of a "very parochial setting." Despite the fact that Machin cannot truly be a tragic figure, because he is "too close to the earth" and he lacks "poise and natural mobility," Anderson has managed to "convey the physical impact of pain in a human life." Also praises Anderson's style: "The flashbacks are as adventurous as those in *Hiroshima Mon Amour*; the montage sequences are as startling as those of Pudovkin." He concludes by hoping in his next film that Anderson can escape as Richardson has the "murky blood and strife of the back streets." *This Sporting Life* makes him one of "Europe's leading directors."

85. Callenbach, Ernest. Review of *This Sporting Life. Film Quarterly*, 17 (Summer), 45-48.

Sees the film as the "first British breakthrough into the subjective cinema, the cinema which escapes the usual narrative conventions, since Humphrey Jennings." Arguing against the reviews which appeared in *Movie* (*see* no. 77) and *Films and Filming* (*see* no. 65), he states that the film is not hard to follow because of the flashback sequences, that it is not a study of the north of England nor a portrait of the worker as epic hero. He also refutes the assertions that the film concentrates on homosexuality, nor is it a treatise on the corrupt upper classes. The film is a "portrait of a miserable neurotic impasse, from approximately Machin's point of view." In addition, he finds the film richly ambiguous and human in its portrayal of the central character. And in spite of the flaws he finds in the spider scene and the restaurant debacle, Callenbach finds the film "lively and innovative as the New Wave."

86. Cowie, Peter. "An Interview with Lindsay Anderson." *Film Quarterly*, 17, no. 4 (Summer), 12-14.

Discusses British cinema with Anderson after the release of his first feature, *This Sporting Life*. Anderson talks about the "working class" tone of the film and the tradition-bound studio system in Britain which stifles any film except the obviously middle class one. Films like *This Sporting Life* have helped to open up the British cinema. He also talks about the evolution of his cinematic style from the early Humphrey Jennings-inspired documentaries *Wakefield Express* and *Every Day Except Christmas*. Anderson denies that the style of *This Sporting Life* was borrowed from Renais.

1965

87. Mekas, Jonas. "On Ugliness and Art." *Village Voice*, 7 (1 August), 13.
     Describes Anderson as being "finished before he started making" *This Sporting Life*. He sees only ugliness in the film, no love or compassion, just hate and anger. He feels that Anderson did not get close to his subject nor did he get into it. It has nothing to do with art.

88. Stephenson, Ralph and J. R. Debrix. *The Cinema as Art*. Baltimore, Md. Penguin Books, pp. 41, 244.
     References to some camera angles used in *This Sporting Life* in order to depict the football players as "black brutal giants."

1966

89. Gray, Paul. "Class Theatre, Class Film: An Interview with Lindsay Anderson." Edited by Kelly Morris. *Tulane Drama Review*, 11 (Fall), 122-129.
     Anderson discusses British film: "We haven't had filmmakers with the creative independence of directors like Antonioni and Fellini, or Godard and Renais." On the other hand, "British films tend to be less esoteric—we have a strong tradition of social responsibility." Anderson also discusses the middle class film which has dominated the English cinema for so long and the emergence of lower-class properties like *This Sporting Life* in the middle 50s through the early 60s. He also briefly talks about the relationship between his film work and theater work. He likes controlled and rhythmic form which makes his theater work "cinematic," or makes his films "theatrical."

90. Kauffmann, Stanley. *A World on Film: Criticism and Comment*. New York: Harper & Row, pp. 209-212.
     Reprint of his review of *This Sporting Life* (*see* no. 75).

91. Kelly, Terence with Graham Norton and George Perry. *A Competitive Cinema*. London: The Institute of Economic Affairs, Ltd., pp. 3, 160.
     Refers to Anderson's connections with the British New Wave and to the Experimental Film Fund.

92. Manvell, Roger. *New Cinema in Europe*. London: Studio Vista Limited, pp. 115, 130, 131.
     Minor references to *Every Day Except Christmas* and the British Film Institute's Experimental Film Fund. Also a brief discussion of *This Sporting Life* which is described as penetrating the surface likenesses of reality to "explore inner motivation, enlarging nature in the process and developing actuality into metaphor, as in the violent gladiatorial rugby football sequences." It is called the most "advanced film that Britain has so far made."

1967

93. Anon. Interview with Lindsay Anderson. *Cinema International*, no. 16, pp. 685-690.

This article in French contains two interviews with the "founders" of the Free Cinema movement, Lindsay Anderson and Karel Reisz. The interview is a general one in which Anderson is asked how he came to films, making them, and writing about them. He is also asked some questions about his response to schools of filmmakers, and the problems between commercial and personal success in the film world.

1968

94. Coleman, John. "Big Tati." *New Statesman*, 76 (19 July), 89-90
Brief review of *The White Bus*, describing it as an "ill-fated" episode of the three-part Delaney film. The reviewer found pointless the heavy-handed "fun at the expense of bigotry, and an intermittent adoption of colour."

95. Gessner, Robert. *The Moving Image.* New York: E. P. Dutton & Company, Inc., p. 52.
This Sporting Life is cited as an example of the thematic freedom which was achieved by the British films which used "sharp social analysis" to critique the Establishment and the status quo.

96. Gifford, Denis. *British Cinema.* New York: A. S. Barnes & Company, p. 9.
This encyclopedia entry lists a partial biography and filmography through 1969.

97. Gow, Gordon. Review of *The White Bus. Films and Filming*, 14. no. 12 (September), 42.
Despite the provincial setting of Shelagh Delaney's story, *The White Bus* has a "universality that stems immediately from its succinct opening phases." This review, which focuses mainly on recounting the episodes which make up the film, praises Anderson's satire of contemporary life which remains crisp if not fresh after the three year delay in the public showing of the film. Sees the ending as suggesting that "[n]ostalgia is a snare: the narrow concepts of living that the girl had fled from, and the futility of looking back for anything other than affirmation that the move she made was in the right direction, are restated in a neat little coda, both funny and sad, which takes place at closing time in a fish-and-chips shop."

98. Marowitz, Charles and Simon Trussler, eds. *Theatre at Work: Playwrights and Productions in the Modern British Theatre.* With an Introduction by Irving Wardle. New York: Hill and Wang, pp. 81, 83, 92.
Brief account of Arnold Wesker's relationship with Anderson. On several occasions he asked Anderson to read stories he had written as possible film ideas. Anderson agreed but, for a variety of reasons, Wesker did not send him anything until he had finished his play, "Chicken Soup." Anderson read the piece and wanted to do it at the Royal Court. It was not done there but eventually was produced.

99 Millar, Daniel. Review of *The White Bus. Sight and Sound*, 37, no. 4 (Autumn), 205-206.
Sees *The White Bus* "as a fascinating experiment if not exactly an interesting, still less a successful, film." Made from one of Shelagh Delaney's "feeble little sketches," the film goes far beyond the boundaries of the original, thanks largely

to Delaney's script, but loses unity in the process. Anderson takes the admixture of documentary and fantasy already in the original sketch and transforms it into a "much more ambitious and sweeping statement about the quality of modern life in the English industrial conurbations, as seen through alienated eyes." The director, by reducing everything to parody, undercuts the affirmation present in other films. The review concludes: "An ambitious and experimental failure by Lindsay Anderson is better worth watching than a boring 'success' by most other British directors. But his admirers, like Oliver Twist, will continue to ask for more."

100. Millar, Gavin. Review of *If... Sight and Sound*, 38, no. 1 (Winter), 42-43.
    Millar, in looking for something "prophetic, cryptic, poetic, transforming," all traits which he feels Anderson wants for the film, finds the film flawed, out of balance, a mishmash of styles and intentions. Anderson ignores his real gifts as a documentarist in a "whirlwind of styles." The balance of fine scenes, beautifully photographed, is lost "in the headlong drive to the end." Finally we, as the audience, struggle to find ourselves in the film. Where do we stand in relation to the youthful revolutionaries? Perhaps in front of their guns.

101. Mortimer, Penelope. "Anderson's Masterwork." *The Observer Review* (22 December), p. 19.
    Finds *If...* a masterwork, in spite of the fact that on first viewing she was disturbed by the ending (on second viewing she felt its inevitability). She singles out the "transfusion" of fantasy and reality as being so skillfully done that for a large part of the film there is no dividing line between the two. "This is as near a true representation of life as you can get." In art, she notes, "it is a waste of time to try to differentiate between the two."

102. Powell, Dilys. "Much Virtue in *If*." *Sunday Times* (London) (22 December), p. 24.
    Describes *If...* as an extraordinary film; well-made, with fine camera work and excellent acting. It was only on second viewing, however, that she saw the progression from the "opening hilarities to the explosive ending." On her second viewing, everything slid into place, and the ending became inevitable. She cautions her readers to avoid taking the film literally and to enjoy the movement from episode to episode which results in violent conclusion.

103. Robinson, David. "Anderson Shooting *If....*" *Sight and Sound*, 37, no. 3 (Summer), 130-131.
    A rather informal account of some of the incidents Anderson had while shooting *If....* Discusses the extras for the final showdown scene who seem to have gotten into the spirit of making the film, the technical details of shooting the toilet scene, a brief encounter sparked by the long days of shooting. Finds this film quite different from Anderson's earlier intense and lyrical documentaries or the "sombre tragedy" of *This Sporting Life*. Anderson understands this film to be an extension of the technique he developed for *The White Bus*, in which he used an extremely simple shooting style. It was a reaction against the over-application of technique which seems more and more to him as a "kind of mannerism as opposed to a genuine style."

104. Sarris, Andrew. *The American Cinema-Directors and Directions 1929-1968.* New York: E. P. Dutton and Company, Inc., p. 206.

Contains a partial filmography and evaluation of Anderson. Describes him as a "leading luminary of the *Sequence-Sight-and-Sound* generation of the late forties and early fifties," who has striven in his films "to express a subtle, supple, and highly individualized sensibility."

105. Schillaci, Anthony. *Movies and Morals.* Notre Dame, Ind.: Fides Publishers, Inc., pp. 151, 171.

Describes *This Sporting Life* as a film about an "aggressive athlete's unthinking passion for a widow [which] proves once more that each man destroys the thing he loves, and in so doing, destroys himself."

106. Schrader, P. Review of *If....* *Cinema,* 5, no. 3, pp. 46-47.

The trouble with *If...*, this critic says, is that Anderson wanted to portray "the poetry of violence" and ended by creating a movie for the youth mass-cult, thereby making it "imminently sellable." In spite of the film's obvious achievements, it falls prey to "twisted intentions, and dashed ambitions." The audience, however, cannot accuse Anderson of pretentiousness, just confusion: "Anderson's poetry creates bafflement rather than involvement." Sees the film as an attempt to recreate Jean Vigo's 1932 film *Zéro de Conduite* and in so doing the director aspired to the highest echelons of film art. "Unfortunately, Anderson's surrealistic details miss the mark."

107. S[hivas], M[ark]. Review of *If....* *Movie,* 16 (Winter), 39.

Lindsay Anderson has a lot of fun with the school system, "catching its cruelties and lunacies with exact observation." The reviewer is not sure what Anderson has done, but he appears to be "firing at several targets at once, talking about English society and conduct in general, and he is interestingly ambivalent toward attitudes and ways of life he obviously finds both attractive and repellent."

108. Sussex, Elizabeth. "Lindsay Anderson's New Film." The *Times* (London) (29 November), p. 14.

Consists mostly of Anderson's observations about *If...*, noting the prophetic nature of the film coming as it did on the heels of the student revolution of the sixties, although Anderson points out that the film was made well in advance of the current upheaval, and the script begun some ten years prior to the actual shooting. Anderson does not feel that the film is an incitement to riot because it is anarchistic rather than revolutionary. For him, anarchism demands the highest value for personal responsibility.

109. Thomas, Bob, ed. *Directors in Action.* New York: The Bobbs-Merrill Company, Inc., p. 213.

In an interview with the director Paul Williams, Anderson mentions trying to capture the musical qualities of telling a story.

1969

110. Alpert, Hollis. "Fall of the British Establishment." *Saturday Review,* 52 (15 February), 50.

Finds *If...* ultimately puzzling because of a loss of "causality." He likes the sharply observed details and the good acting "(no 'names' of any consequence, by the way)," and the fascinating, if often repellant, material. A lack of perspective, the mingling of fact and fantasy, and a lack of clarity, however, leave the audience with a Chinese puzzle. "A comment in itself, perhaps," Alpert notes.

111. Anon. Review of *If....* *Filmfacts,* 12; 73.

Contains the usual synopsis, credits, critique, and sampling of film reviews. The critical consensus of the reviews was: eight favorable, seven mixed, and one negative.

112. Armstrong, Marion. "Bloody Rebellion." *Christian Century,* 86 (2 July), 905-906.

If... is described as "adroit and sharp as cold steel," a film, however, which has lost its "furiously satiric edge and therefore some of its dramatic thrust" since the events of Cornell where guns were actually brandished.

113. Arnold, Gary. "'If...': Pop Rebellion Fantasy, and Snob Appeal." *The Washington Post* (13 June), p. G3.

Arnold finds this film too filled with references to other directors and other movies, a consequence he thinks of Anderson's past as a film critic. The tone of *If...* is also a "bit too shrewd and calculating to convince us that the action is 'realistic'" Even though the early scenes are beautifully done, it is the "romanticizing of the youth-as-guerrilla" which accounts for the film's appeal. Finally, he sees the film as positing two alternatives for youth to become: "cold-blooded hypocrites or cold-blooded nihilists." While he doubts Anderson would care to defend this thesis, it is fanning the "flames of that hot box office."

114. Baker, Russell. "Observer: Youth Without Rose-Colored Glasses." *The New York Times* (13 May), p. 46.

In this "editorial," Russell Baker defends *If...* against the onslaught of letter writers who are complaining about the film's "revolutionary" message. Baker says the film isn't "about" anything but that it is beautifully made and, despite its "foreignness" for American viewers, conjures up the lost world of adolescence by chucking the "bogus romantic memory of childhood which adults carry about as part of their conversational baggage."

115. Canby, Vincent. "British Film Breaks Hold on Cannes Fete." *The New York Times* (26 May), p. 56.

A news story which notes that *If...* had just received the Golden Palm at Cannes, breaking the domination of major prizes by Continental European films. In spite of the fact that *If...* had received a rather cool reception from the French press and that the favorite French entry was *Z,* directed by Costa-Gavras, Anderson's film won the prize. Apparently there was considerable jockeying on the jury before *If...* won. This year for the first time the jury was not dominated by French members. Bo Widerberg's film *Adalen 31* received second prize after its first round votes went to *If...*; *Z* was awarded third prize.

116. Canby, Vincent. "Give Me Back My Yo-Yo." *The New York Times* (10 March), pp. 1, 35.

Canby describes *If...* as "such a precisely documented satire, so firmly grounded in the reality of dumb, institutionalized horrors, that its moments of surreal fantasy seem to have been stuck into it like maraschino cherries into a loaf of protein bread." The reviewer also mentions *The Singing Lesson* and *The White Bus,* a movie which is "an austere, caustic view of a semi-socialist state, seen through the wide-angle eyes of a young girl who is a writer." In *The White Bus,* Anderson is "a marvelously gifted, passionately concerned, moviemaker who is trying very hard to free himself from the restrictions of the visible world that can no longer satisfy his sense of the absurd."

117. Canby, Vincent. "The Importance of Being Oscar." *The New York Times* (20 April), Section II, p. 8D.

Brief discussion of the censorship problems that two short scenes of frontal nudity in *If...* caused for Anderson and Paramount. They wanted an "R" rating rather than an "X" rating. Canby notes that the movie is "politically rather than sexually provocative," and that there are films of far more prurient interest which have earned an "R" rating. He concludes by noting that any "rating system as flexible as this one can't be all bad."

118. Cecil, Norman. Review of *If....Films in Review,* 20, no. 4 (April), 255-256.

The reviewer describes the film as "psychotic" and the script as full of "sick and second-hand imaginings." He sees Anderson as extolling "things centuries of human experience have invalidated (uncontrolled adolescence, homosexuality, amorality, anarchy)."

119. Cocks, Jay. "*If* Does Not Equal Zero." *Time,* 93 (21 March), 97.

Cocks unfavorably compares *If...* with *Zero for Conduct* finding a number of specific elements present in both, including the climactic scene. Unfortunately, *Zero* succeeds where *If...* does not. Although the film is "occasionally powerful and moving," it is never more than "forceful and faintly mannered prose." Anderson's sense of place makes "College House so horrifyingly tangible that it becomes the main character in the film," but his sense of fantasy is not as "acute." The confusion between reality and fantasy "suspends disbelief without enriching the narrative." Finally *If...* "badly needs and sadly lacks the sort of lyricism that Vigo brought to *Zero.*"

120. Corliss, Richard. "Hollywood and the Student Revolt." *National Review,* 21 (17 June), 606.

Corliss finds this film failing to match up with *This Sporting Life.* It lacks intelligence, direction, finesse, and control. There's an irony in the ending; "instead of the school falling apart, the film does." The reviewer sees Anderson's ambition as killing *If....* "What could have been an anarchic work of art, if told realistically, was turned by the unnecessary shuffling of tenses, moods and colors into an elaborate but unsuccessful *coup.*"

121. Craddock, John. "*If*... High School Unless." *Film Society Review,* 5, no. 1 (September), 30-38.

In this review, which compares Frederick Wiseman's *High School, U.S.A.* with *If...,* the reviewer explores the discipline and educational excellence of the English public school with the banality and boredom of Wiseman's high school. Both educational institutions are open to satire and criticism; Anderson by extending his criticism to include open revolt (imagined or real) on the part of the students has suggested a possible outcome for the repressive methods of the

English boarding school. Craddock does criticize the ending of *If . . .* as providing a dissipation of the tension which has been built up during the film by reducing the continuous shooting to the level of a TV western. The final shot of Mick firing away becomes anti-climàctic because it is an ending which is impossible to resolve.

122. Dempsey, Michael. Review of *If . . . . Film Heritage,* 5, no. 1 (Fall), 13-20.

In spite of what the reviewer sees as "patchy, obscure, muddled elements" which cloud our view of the rebels, *If . . .* remains a "cool, distanced, and very funny film" which ridicules the dissidents as well as the society from which they come. Unlike Jean Vigo's *Zero for Conduct, If . . .* has an objective point of view (at least most of the time it does) which allows Anderson to be critical of everything he portrays. The reviewer also points out the ambivalence Anderson shows toward the school he is using for a backdrop. The visual recreation of the college, with its well-kept lawns, stained glass windows, and hewn stone, are "redolent of a tradition that valued reason and calm and did not in its halcyon days make them euphemisms for inflexibility and stagnancy." Anderson discovers "beauty in what he might like to demolish."

123. Ebert, Roger. "Students vs. the System in Bloody Vision." *Chicago Sun Times* (1 June), section II, pp. 5, 8.

Instead of making an upper-class *Loneliness of a Long Distance Runner,* Anderson, by using sharply defined vignettes, builds the story of three rebels in their public school through a series of sections, each one becoming more fantastic in content and style until the whole film erupts in an orgy of violence at the end. Anderson keeps suggesting that "if" the pressures and obtuseness of the school system were to build up to such an extent, just this sort of rebellion might take place. Ebert finds this film not only timely, given the rebellion on American campuses, but also the best film so far that year, a film which not only was relevant for the youth of today but one which will stand up 20 years from now.

124. Farber, Stephen. "Before the Revolution." *Hudson Review,* 22 (Autumn), 469-476.

Focuses on Anderson's "skeptical consideration of the student rebel." Farber sees the film mocking both the antagonists in "the battle at Generation Gap." In spite of the fact that the institution is responsible for creating the boys, the boys nevertheless exhibit a pettiness and destructiveness more adolescent than revolutionary. Anderson has captured the "insolent charm, the arrogance, contemptuousness, and fundamental *narrowness* of so many young rebels." *If . . .* also is a film about "subtler distortions of reality, the way in which we make slight adjustments in our perceptions to satisfy our fantasy images of ourselves."

125. Gladwell, David. "Editing Anderson's *If . . .*" *Screen,* 10, no. 1 (January-February), 24-33.

An informal article on both the art of editing in general and on the joys and frustrations of working with Lindsay Anderson. Gladwell points out how much control over the film, every aspect of it, Anderson demands. He also comments briefly on the director's filming style, rather old-fashioned with precise camera setups and camera movements carefully rehearsed. His meticulous attention to detail included the tinkering with the Master Track several weeks after the final mixing.

126. Gow, Gordon. Review of *If . . . . Films and Filming*, 15, no. 6 (March), 50-51.

The virtues of *If . . .* are that Anderson has taken a tired theme and treated it with a freshness and an intelligent ambivalence, "which is to say a mind that refuses to reduce complexities to 'cut-and-dried' propaganda." Even Anderson's defects are seen as virtues: "The establishment is rebuked through satire, which is lumbered occasionally with the heavy emphasis of an artist so deeply sincere that he wants to be absolutely certain that people will get the point." Using a style both flexible and confident, Anderson develops the story of a rebel leader "who, in his quest for freedom, has permitted himself to indulge the lust for power, demolishing one establishment to replace it with another. . . ."

127. Hartung, Philip T. "If Youth But Knew." *Commonweal*, 90 (21 March), 21-22.

The reviewer places *If . . .* among the current spate of "youth cycle" films and finds it one of the best. In this handsomely photographed film Anderson combines realism, surrealism, and flights of fantasy to capture the world of boys dominated by an establishment "smothered in tradition and clichés." Hartung even sees the unprepared-for ending as coming off because the film "is so fascinating as it runs from scene to scene and so skillfully directed by Anderson that we sit stunned at the end, whether or not we are supposed to accept what happens as real or imaginary."

128. Houston, Penelope. "Ifs and Buts at Cannes." *The Spectator*, no. 222 (30 May), 728-729.

Review of the happenings at the Cannes Film Festival with a brief mention of Anderson's *If . . .*, which was the official British entry. The festival seemed rather placid after the turmoil of the year before.

129. Johnson, Albert. Review of *If . . . . Film Quarterly*, 22, no. 4 (Summer), 48-52.

"*If . . .* is one of the most extraordinary studies of adolescence and education in the history of the motion picture. . . ." Johnson feels that this film more than confirms Lindsay Anderson's genius as a director. "If there had ever been any doubt that Lindsay Anderson's second feature would surpass any of the recent films made in Great Britain, . . . then the time has come for suspension of doubt and acknowledgement of his genius." The reviewer sees Anderson as both repelled and fascinated by the rebels and using the fantasy sequences of anarchy as "ferocious warnings" for the modern world.

130. Kael, Pauline. "School Days, School Days." *The New Yorker*, 45 (15 March), 152, 154, 159-161.

Kael begins her criticism of *If . . .* by discussing the hype job the advertising people did to sell the film to "youth." She spends the best part of the rest of the review unfavorably comparing *If . . .* with Jean Vigo's 1933 classic about a schoolboy's revolt, *Zero for Conduct*. Despite the unity given to the film by Anderson's "tone of cold, seething anger," the "picture is clogged by all the difficult, ambitious things he attempts and flubs." The film has a "bleak, pseudo-documentary solemnity that is about as attractive to Americans as to have blood pudding." Kael is critical of Anderson's dehumanization of the establishment which makes them so easy to kill and which is based on the inconsistent and ambivalent feelings of children. If Vigo did not confuse a child's view of the world with reality, Anderson does, and therein lies the problem.

131. Kauffmann, Stanley. Review of *If... New Republic,* 160 (15 February), 22.

Kauffmann admires Anderson's talent but finds both of his early feature films, *If...* and *This Sporting Life,* to be serious disappointments. Despite passages of "extraordinary beauty—not only visually but in concept, editing, and rhythm," he finds the dissipation toward the end of *If...* even more marked than in *This Sporting Life.* The opening of the film with its "quasi-Brechtian approach" is quite exciting "as all the cinematic elements are used with great skill by a real mind with a real view." It is primarily the quirky plot sequences which wrenched the film out of the "varyingly successful 'documentation'" of the first half of the film and which introduced the grotesqueries which ultimately lead up to what Kauffmann describes as Anderson's unsyntactical and ruinous finish.

132. Kotlowitz, Robert. "Aspects of Love." *Harpers,* 238 (April), 115-116.

Kotlowitz sees the film *If...* as a "sardonic and powerful movie, rich in detail, filled with anger and horror at any authoritarian attempt to manipulate or diminish humanity." Anderson has constructed the school to mean "far more than the sum of its eccentric particularities"; college becomes England itself, "perfidious Albion in the smothering embrace of bourgeois smugness." Despite all of the good things about the film, it fails to carry the weight of the meaning Anderson assigns to it. "All the Crusader ironies will not hold, nor will the self-conscious, muscle-flexing revolutionary fervor which almost capsizes the movie at the end. *If...* is really about the psychosis of revenge while it romantically pretends to be about considerably more."

133. MacDonald, Dwight. *Dwight MacDonald on Movies.* Englewood Cliffs, N.J.: Prentice-Hall, Inc., pp. 395-396.

MacDonald sees the British realist drama as having created a low-life stereotype quite as boring as the predictable high-life "irrealism" it replaced. He describes the drama of *This Sporting Life* as a doggedly grim story directed by a filmmaker as avisual as Tony Richardson, one who "tries to conceal the fact by using cinematic 'effects' where they are not needed or are positively destructive." He sees no reason except for an effect "at *nouvelle-vague* smartness" why the opening of the film should be told in flashback. He also faults Anderson's camera as being either "too flatly, clutteredly realistic" or else "too 'indicative.'" Finally MacDonald feels that Anderson and Reisz threw in the "class struggle partly to pile on the agony: Free Cinema is decently depressing. And partly from sheer habit: Free Cinema is socially conscious."

134. Manvell, Roger. *New Cinema in Britain.* New York: E. P. Dutton, pp. 48-51 and passim.

Several references to Anderson's documentaries, *Wakefield Express, O Dreamland Thursday's Children,* and *Every Day Except Christmas,* plus some discussion of *This Sporting Life* as a movement forward for the British film. It was not merely a realistic study of a rugby player, but also of a man with both extraordinary power and aggressiveness as well as sensitivity. There is also a brief mention of *The White Bus* as part of a trilogy which had received only sporadic exposure in the exhibition halls.

135. Mekas, Jonas. "Free Cinema and the New Wave," in *The Emergence of Film Art*. Edited by Lewis Jacobs. New York: Hopkinson and Blake, p. 400.

Reprint of an article appearing in *Film Culture* (*see* no. 55).

136. Morganstern, Joseph. "School Days." *Newsweek*, 73 (31 March), 95-96.

Morganstern begins his review with: "The very crudity that may disqualify Lindsay Anderson's *If...* as an enduring piece of work also makes it an exciting entertainment of the moment." Unfortunately, the reviewer goes on to pillory Anderson for the many failures of the film. The rebels are "[p]redatory, humorless and despicable as the cardboard creeps who goad them into rebelling." Unlike Jean Vigo's *Zero for Conduct*, this film lacks joy and gaiety, even "genuine, outright malevolence." There are fine scenes, though, and Miroslav Ondricek's color photography "makes everything look good."

137. Prima, Jesse. Review of *If....* *Cineaste*, 11, no. 4 (Spring), 19-20.

Sees the adolescent rebels as progressing from non-conformity to dissent to protest to resistance and finally to armed struggle. The problem with the film, however, is that Anderson has stacked the deck in favor of the law and order system in spite of the apparent sympathy in the film for the youthful rebellion. "For to pose the 'revolution' this way is to conclude that one must support either a moribund social structure or a self-defeating adventurist rebellion." The audience will then associate all "protest with foolish adventurism" and thus reject the possibility of unity among dissident groups. The film is the "ideological first cousin to that American neofascist atrocity," *Wild in the Streets*.

138. Reif, Tony. Review of *If....* *Take One*, 2, no. 2, p. 21.

In discussing the ambiguous fantasy of the film, the author finally acknowledges that it is not important whether or not what we are seeing on the screen is supposed to be real or not; the whole point of the film is that it is meant to symbolize a kind of social order. The school, the final rebellious act of the dissident boys, the particular incidents of the drama itself need not be taken literally. In fact it is the very state of uncertainty which keeps the viewer off balance and which provides the film with tension. "As the realistic jostles the stylized and slips into the absurd, the viewer must decide for himself where the likely becomes the unlikely." The often intensely observed realism of school life firmly underpins the satire and caricature, providing the film with "a controlled power, where the two opposing creative directions—intellect and emotion, understanding and involvement—are united...."

139. Schickel, Richard. "Angry Knot in the Old School Tie." *Life*, 66 (28 February), 8.

According to the theories of film which this reviewer holds, *If...* should not hold together, but it does, "angry, tough and full of sting." It is an exploration of the "fantasies of escape, rebellion and destruction shared by the school's three least tractable scholars." It is a vision, and "like all good visions there is nothing escapist or comforting about it." Even though Anderson seems to be borrowing avant-garde techniques to "revitalize material that is excessively familiar," he does not slip into Godard's trap of creating characters who are merely "abstractions, intellectual constructs, designed to help him illustrate philosophical theories." Instead, he reveals the public school's character "simply by letting his camera prowl its corridors and rooms, precisely and economically presenting the evidence of its seedy and irrelevant traditionalism."

140. Schlesinger, Arthur Jr. "*If*...'Brilliant and Disturbing.'" *Vogue,* 153 (15 March), 40.

"*If*... is a brilliant and disturbing film. The director, Lindsay Anderson, sees the school, with its structure of irrational power, as a microcosm of society." Schlesinger puts the film in the context of other British schoolboy studies from *Tom Brown's Schooldays* to the present. There is a difference, though. With clinical detachment, Anderson explores the inhumanity of the institution unleavened by sentiment or geniality.

141. Shalit, Gene. "Go!—for the Fury, Force, and Fun of *If*...." *Look,* 33 (18 March), 84.

"*If*... is outrageous— a movie so brilliant, so special that it's dangerous to write about." Gene Shalit likes just about everything in the film; the script "a mix of terror and humor," the cast "extraordinary," and the photography "immaculate." Lindsay Anderson compresses it all until "they explode in your face."

142. Shalit, Gene. Review of *If*.... *Ladies Home Journal,* 86, no. 4 (April), 12.

Shalit finds the film profound, "with enormous power. If we get one film to *equal* it this year, we'll all be very lucky indeed." He says the lack of familiar faces on the screen adds to the film's strength.

143 Sherwin, David and Lindsay Anderson. *If...: A Film by Lindsay Anderson and David Sherwin.* New York: Simon and Schuster, 167 pp.

Screenplay of the film.

144. Spiers, David. Review of *If*.... *Screen,* 10, no. 2 (March-April), 85-89.

Anderson, using a style "bare, stripped to its essentials," provides the audience with his detailed social observation in an unobtrusive manner. The story is basically one of a group of rebellious schoolboys who will no longer conform to the mindless and now meaningless traditions of their boarding school. Mick and his friends come to symbolize pure feelings and instincts in an atmosphere which does everything to stifle them. Spiers points out the various hypocrisies of the place, from the quasi-liberal headmaster who spouts platitudes about traditions and service to the bullying and sexually repressed members of the house. It is a society in which instinctual feelings have no place. The hero of this film echoes Frank Machin's frustrations by restricting his responses to society to physical terms. The reviewer does introduce a curious note at the end of the review when he mentions that by elevating pure instincts *per se* in the violent conclusion to the film, Anderson seems to be providing a fascist implication to the film, and coming from someone who has always been aligned with the Left, it is a curious fact indeed.

145. Storey, David. *In Celebration.* New York: Grove Press, 103 pp.

The play which Anderson filmed.

146. Sussex, Elizabeth. *Lindsay Anderson.* New York: Praeger, 95 pp.

This is the first full-length study of Anderson. The author covers his early documentaries, his crusading period during the Free Cinema movement, and, of course, the later films: *This Sporting Life, The White Bus, The Singing Lesson,* and *If*.... Also included is a filmography complete through 1968.

147. Young, Vernon. "Film Chronicle: Notes on the Compulsive Revolution." *Hudson Review,* 22 (Winter), 649-650.

Young sees *If*... guided by "class hatred" and flawed by a lack of purpose and an overuse of trendy cinematic devices. He liked the first half of the film greatly but found the shift to the dreamlike sequences confusing. A member of the Cannes audience described the film as helping her to understand why the British were "so arrogant and stupid." Young hoped she was referring to Anderson.

1970

148. Cowie, Peter. Review of *If*.... *International Film Guide,* 7: 106-107.

If... is "much the richest and most poetic film to come from an English director during the Sixties." It is the story of three adolescents in "the process of 'discovering' life." Anderson focuses on an English boarding school as a mirror of English society where much of "the ceremonial is utterly at odds with natural behavior, and the extraordinary contradictions within the public school are repeated at every level of English society. *If*... is a film that takes these anomalies seriously by mocking them, is a film that captures all the strange, often lyrical elements of hero worship and adolescence."

149. Crist, Judith. *The Private Eye, the Cowboy and the Very Naked Girl.* New York: Holt, Rinehart and Winston, pp. 25, 39, 40, 59.

Several passing references to *This Sporting Life* as a viciously realistic film which probes "the inarticulate animal that walks among men."

150. Flatley, Guy." 'Home': The Playwright:'I never saw a Pinter Play.' " *The New York Times* (29 November), Section II, p. 1.

In this interview with Anderson and David Storey on the occasion of the New York opening of Storey's play "Home," which was directed by Anderson, Anderson is described as a "47 year old, brilliant bachelor with a genius for the theatrical, a penchant for the put down, and no reputation whatever for reticence." While the article does not deal directly with Anderson's film work, it does give insight into him as a man and his working relationship with Storey which, for his film career as well as his career as a director of plays, has been important.

151. Gelmis, Joseph. "Lindsay Anderson," in *The Film Director as Superstar.* Garden City, N.Y.: Doubleday & Company, Inc., pp. 93-110.

This interview begins with a brief biography and filmography. Anderson discusses how he became a film director, some of his ideas on film editing, and gives a rather extended treatment of *If*.... He also talks about his tendency to alternate between the poetic and the satiric as, for example, in *Every Day Except Christmas* and *O Dreamland.* This same tendency has spilled over into his feature films, especially in *If*..., where fantasy and realism mix without the usual separation. This technique allows the audience a greater imaginative freedom.

152. Halliwell, Leslie. *Filmgoer's Companion.* Third edition. New York: Hill

and Wang, p. 43.
Encyclopedia entry with filmography.

153.　Jacobs, Lewis. "Directors Speak," in *The Movies as Medium*. New York: Farrar, Strauss, & Giroux, p. 3.
Brief quote from Anderson's article "Creative Elements" (*see* no. 360).

154.　Kael, Pauline. *Going Steady*. Boston: Little, Brown and Company, pp. 279-286.
Reprint of "School Days, School Days" (*see* no. 130).

155.　Kael, Pauline. "School Days, School Days," in *Film 69/70: An Anthology by the National Society of Film Critics*. Edited by Joseph Morganstern and Stefan Kanfer. New York: Simon and Schuster, pp. 84-90.
Reprint of earlier review of *If . . .* (*see* no. 130).

156.　Kauffmann, Stanley. Review of "Home." *New Republic*, 163 (12 December), 20, 33.
This theater review mentions his reservations about Anderson's work as a film director, an "unusual directing talent even when these films go structurally awry." Anderson's theater work provides the critic with the answer he has been seeking. Anderson needs greater shape to the projects he undertakes, and with this drama he is the interpreter, not the shaper.

157.　S., P.H. "The Times Diary: BFI: *Sight and Sound*, and Fury." *The Times* (London) (26 September), p 12.
A news item mentioning the resignation of Anderson and Karel Reisz from the British Film Institute over the institute's insistence that the board of governors assume an internal rather than an external inquiry into the BFI's role in the 1970s. The notice also mentions how the directors had been frustrated by the institute's bureaucratic machinery when trying to get reforms pushed through. They had gotten *Sight and Sound* and *The Monthly Film Bulletin* to reverse their editorial policies in favor of more coverage of British films. Others were also considering resigning in protest as well.

158.　Stanhope, Henry. "East End Film With Local Teenage Cast Finds National Distribution." *The Times* (London) (21 August), p. 4
Anderson is quoted in this news item about the reception of *Bronco Bullfrog*. He found the film to have a special poetic quality not usually present in British films. It was a film "not just promising but a promise fulfilled."

159.　Willis, John. "*If . . . .*" *Screen World*. New York: Crown Publishers, pp. 154-55.
Contains a partial filmography and photography from *If . . . .*

1971

160.　Anon. "Biofilmographie—Lindsay Anderson." *Avant-Scene in Cinema*, no. 119 (November), 58.
Brief biography and filmography in French of Anderson's film work up through *If . . . .*

161. Anon. "The Times Diary: *If...* Trio Turn to Candide." The *Times* (London) (11 May), p. 13.

An announcement that Anderson is working on a new film (*O Lucky Man!*) with David Sherwin and Malcolm McDowell, and that he would not discuss it except to say that it was about what happens after school. Anderson is described as "Britain's most talented and individual director." Anderson is quoted as saying that he doesn't see why people feel that films should be made so quickly; a screenplay, for example, should take as long as a novel to write.

162. Anon. "25th Cannes Film Fete Opens With Glitter and Pomp." The *New York Times* (13 May), p. 50.

Brief news item mentioning the opening ceremonies of the 25th Cannes Film Festival, during which Anderson was honored as a film director. The article mentions that Anderson's only two feature films, *This Sporting Life* and *If...*, both won honors at the festival.

163. Butler, Ivan. *The Making of Feature Films: A Guide.* Hammondsworth, England: Penguin Books, Ltd., pp. 62-66 and passim.

Contains some brief references to *If...*, the nudity and location shooting, and reprints the article by the editor David Gladwell on cutting the film (*see* no. 125). There is also an interview with Anderson in the section of the book on The Director, in which he talks about how he goes about shooting a film, whether he prefers location or studio shooting, how detailed he likes his scripts, and so on.

164. Cowie, Peter, ed. *A Concise History of the Cinema Since 1940, Volume 2.* New York: A. S. Barnes and Company, pp. 86-87.

Mentions that Anderson is one of those filmmakers who began as a critic. "He was a key figure in the Free Cinema movement, whose initiators aimed at cheap, non-studio films by creative people, and claimed to be the first generation of British filmmakers to be in control of their material." The concentration on the working class and on contemporary society was reflected in *This Sporting Life, The White Bus* and *If...*.

165. Dickinson, Thorold. *A Discovery of Cinema.* London: Oxford University Press, pp. 138-139.

Dickinson cites *If...* as an example of a film which allowed the director complete control over his material. The movie, without any recognized stars, with an original script, had to be carried by Anderson alone, "a director with a following but no widely popular record." The film was a success after it was run in a local theater in London. It had been presented without the backing of two major circuits in England, but quickly released by one of them after the enthusiastic response of the first viewers and the critics.

166. Issari, M. Ali. *Cinema Verite.* East Lansing, Mich.: Michigan State University Press, pp. 20, 60.

A couple of brief notes on Anderson as one of the founders of the Free Cinema movement in England.

167. Kauffman, Stanley. *Figures of Light: Film Criticism and Comment.* New York: Harper & Row, pp. 134-136.

Reprint of his review of *If...* (*see* no. 131).

168. Levin, G. Roy. *Documentary Explorations: 15 Interviews with Film-makers.* Garden City, N.Y.: Doubleday and Company, Inc., pp. 23, 57-71.

The interview with Anderson centers on his ideas about documentary. He sees the difference between documentary and feature films as a distinct one despite the use of cinema-verité technique in fiction films. "It isn't a question of technique," he says, "it is a question of the material. If the material is actual, then it is documentary. If the material is invented, then it is not documentary...." When discussing the social role of the artist as filmmaker, Anderson responded, "I don't sit down and think, now in the present state of society what should one do. I just think, here I am living from day to day, there are certain possibilities, I wonder what would be the best thing to do next." Also included are some of his ideas about Humphrey Jennings and John Grierson, along with a brief biography of Anderson and an abbreviated filmography with other credits.

169. Mast, Gerald. *A Short History of the Movies.* New York: Bobbs-Merrill, pp. 420 and passim.

Describes Anderson as "the British director most devoted to rebellion against a stagnant and repressive bourgeois society and bourgeois mentality." That rebellion is embodied in the violent central characters of his films and in the violent attacks Anderson makes with his cinematic style by violating the continuity of time, space, and action. The question of his future as a film director lies with whether or not he can "remain free of cliché and his self-conscious film trickery remain fresh and functional."

170. Morella, Joe and Edward Z. Epstein. *Rebels: The Rebel Hero in Films.* New York: The Citadel Press, pp. 152-153.

The chapter on "The British Rebel Heroes" contains some stills from *This Sporting Life.*

171. Rosenthal, Alan. *The New Documentary in Action.* Berkeley: University of California Press, pp. 1, 6, 7.

Several minor references to Anderson: British Free Cinema, *Every Day Except Christmas,* and *Secret People.*

172. Welsh, James E "Bergman and Anderson for Sophomores." *Cinema Journal,* 11, no. 1 (Fall), 52-57.

Contains an analysis of how to use the screenplay of *If...* in a college classroom. The author feels that the students readily responded to the film with "vitality, enthusiasm, and intelligence." The metaphorical violence at the end of the film presented the biggest obstacle to an "intelligent discussion of the film." The central characters were not seen as heroic but rather pathetic, and their crusade as a "flamboyant gesture." The critic liked the detailed camera instructions included in the script which allowed the students to reconstruct accurately the film, a valuable tool for students who are not particularly visually oriented. The screenplay of *If...* may be considered a more detailed analytical tool than most screenplays tend to be.

1972

173. Delson, James. "O Lucky Man!" *Take One,* 3 (May/June), 29-30.

This article contains interviews with three of the main personalities of the film,

Malcolm McDowell, Alan Price, and Lindsay Anderson. The reviewer thinks that the film "is the most meaningful, entertaining and generally overall finest film of 1973." McDowell talks about the genesis of the film script; Price discusses the use of his songs to comment on the action; and Anderson explains the Brechtian alienation within the movie.

174. Giannetti, Louis D. *Understanding Movies.* Englewood Cliffs, N.J.: Prentice-Hall, Inc., p. 190.

Reference to Anderson as part of the neorealist tradition with Richardson and Reisz. The second edition (1972) also briefly discusses the musical devices as well as the movement from fantasy to reality in *O Lucky Man!*

175. Lovell, Alan and Jim Hillier. "Free Cinema," in *Studies in Documentary.* New York: The Viking Press, pp. 133-175.

A rather thorough discussion of the Free Cinema movement and Anderson's role in it. There are analyses of *O Dreamland, Wakefield Express,* and *Every Day Except Christmas* as Anderson's Free Cinema films. The authors also discuss the importance of *Sequence* in the formulation of the tenets of the movement. They include a filmography of the six Free Cinema programs which were run at the National Film Theatre, plus a brief biographical note on the important Free Cinema directors.

176. McKee, Allen. "Why Can't the English Make a Masterpiece?" *The New York Times* (24 December), p. 17.

An article criticizing the British for not producing any masterpieces in film like *Citizen Kane* or *Grand Illusion.* The reviewer sees British films as failing to pay the requisite attention to style with which to put together a classic film. Carol Reed's talent, once established by *Odd Man Out,* has suffered an eclipse because he was unwilling to risk enough to make a really big film. Hitchcock has fallen into repetition, and David Lean into "pointless panorama." Even the new, young directors like Richard Lester, John Schlesinger, and Tony Richardson have not been able to sustain freshness of their early films. Only Lindsay Anderson has "retained his ill-tempered artistry." The author speculates that it is perhaps because he has made so few films that he has not had the time to exorcise his "rebel grumpiness."

177. Mekas, Jonas. "On Ugliness and Art," in *Movie Journal.* New York: The MacMillan Company, p. 90

Reprint of an earlier article (*see* no. 87).

178. Sadoul, Georges. *Dictionary of Film.* Translated, edited, and updated by Peter Morris. Berkeley and Los Angeles: The University of California Press, pp. 154, 374.

Mentions *If...*: "Its anarchic spirit, style of poetic realism, and refusal to compromise stem more from the tradition of Jean Vigo than from that of the British cinema.... it can justly be compared to *Zéro de conduite*—and not to its disfavor."*This Sporting Life* was "a significant breakthrough in the British cinema from the rhetoric and 'objective' social analysis," but it "owes more to French poetic realism and to the style of Central European directors like Wajda."

179. Sadoul, Georges. *A Dictionary of Film Makers.* Translated, edited, and updated by Peter Morris. Berkeley: University of California Press,

(Originally published as *Dictionnaire des Cineastes*, 1965), p. 6.
Partial biography and filmography of Anderson up through *If...*.

180. Schickel, Richard. *Second Sight: Notes on Some Movies, 1965-1970.* New York: Simon and Schuster, pp. 220-222.
Reprint of an earlier review of *If...* for *Life* (*see* no. 139).

181. White, David M. and Richard Averson. *The Celluloid Weapon.* Boston: Beacon Press, p. 56.
Mentions Anderson's monograph on John Ford (*see* no. 434).

182. Young, Vernon. Review of *If...*, in *On Film: Unpopular Essays on a Popular Art.* New York: Quadrangle, pp. 350-351.
Reprint of an earlier article (*see* no. 147).

1973

183. Allombert, Guy. "Le Meilleur des Mondes Possible." *Revue du Cinema/Image et Son,* 273 (June/July), 138-139.
Brief notice of *O Lucky Man!* mentions the connections between Malcolm McDowell's journey and Candide's. Anderson's direction is praised as is the music and McDowell's performance.

184. Alterman, Loraine. "Yes, Rock Can Sometimes Save a Bad Movie." *The New York Times* (8 July), section II, pp. 8, 19.
"If Lindsay Anderson's *O Lucky Man!* proves anything, it's that contemporary rock music can save films as well as the conglomerates that own the film companies." She assumes that Warner Brothers will make more money from the album of Alan Price's music for the film than they will make from the movie itself. She also thinks that the musical score makes a point in 25 minutes that three hours of "cliché-infested" film footage does not. The music is "free of pretense and brimming with energy—two qualities that elude Anderson." The only redeeming factor about the film is the creative use of the score as if it were a Greek chorus, to explain and connect the narrative of the young man in search of his fortune.

185. Ankram, Raymond L. "Filmscore: *O Lucky Man!*", *Canyon Cinema-news,* 415 (September/October), 9.
This brief discussion of the film score describes Alan Price's music as "unquestionably the finest I've heard in years." He finds the score particularly appropriate to the visual content of the film and gives Price an "'A#1+'" rating.

186. Anon. "Lindsay Anderson's New Film." *The Times* (London) (30 March), p. 13.
A short news item announcing that *O Lucky Man!*, Lindsay Anderson's newest film, will represent Great Britain at the Cannes Film Festival in May. The film reunites many of the talents from Anderson's previous film *If...*, which won the Grand Prix four years before.

187. Anon. "Lindsay Anderson's *O Lucky Man!*" *Films and Filming,* 19 (May), 29-33.

A picture essay on the film without text, somewhat tracing the plot and progression of the movie.

188. Anon. "Lindsay Anderson trims *O Lucky Man!*" *Variety*, 271 (13 June), 7.

A short news story describing that Anderson had cut an additional nine minutes from the film down to 166 minutes running time and that Warner Brothers had sent out a letter to the New York critics announcing the fact and including Anderson's remark that the present version was now his "final and definitive version."

189. Anon. Review of *O Lucky Man!*. *Filmfacts*, 16, no. 5, pp. 109-115.

Indispensible collection of credits, synopsis, and critique. The critics were largely in favor of the film (8 favorable, 3 mixed, 3 negative). Included are excerpts from the Los Angeles *Times* (Charles Champlin) (*see* no. 303); the Washington *Post* (Gary Arnold) (*see* no. 193); and *Time Magazine* (Jay Cocks) (*see* no. 204).

190. Anon Review of *O Lucky Man!*. *Variety*, 270 (18 April), 30.

The film is described as "rich" but not "complicated." Anderson seems to be saying that society needs an "interior awareness" before the call to change which he sounded in *If...* can be heeded. Both the versatility of the actors and the "notable addition" of the score by Alan Price are singled out for praise. The reviewer finds the film Anderson's attempt to enlighten us all. "Maybe a work of art cannot change things, he seems to intimate, but it can lead to awareness."

191. Anon. "The Artist as Monster." *Time*, 102 (23 July), 87-88.

O Lucky Man! reveals much of Anderson's "dour, sardonic Scots heritage" in its reflection of reality as "grotesque fantasy." He "rages in his films at the state of modern humanity, deadened by conformity and isolated in a world gone ludicrously amuck." The job his films carry out is "to jolt his viewers awake." The duty of the artist is to be a monster, "to aim beyond the limits of tolerance." The article contains a brief biography and synopsis of Anderson's work concluding with Anderson's denial that *O Lucky Man!* will be his last film.

192. Anon. "What's New at the Movies?" *The New York Times* (24 June), p. 16.

Brief notices of *O Lucky Man!* mentioning the reviewers' reactions to the film: seven favorable, seven mixed, and five negative.

193. Arnold, Gary. "A Satirical Tale of Getting Ahead." *The Washington Post* (20 June), p. 11B.

This review begins: "Unless Lindsay Anderson manages to make another movie fast, 'O Lucky Man!' now at the Cinema, should hold up as the prestige bumbler of 1973." He finds this film as well as *If...* "preemptory, nasty, self-important." Arnold calls the film derivative and, despite the fact that Anderson is a "knowledgeable and technically accomplished director," he is "incapable of spontaneous or original effects." His movies reflect "an increasing taste for caricature and fantastic forms of stylization along with an exaggerated sense of their own moral and artistic importance."

194. Barsam, Richard M. *Nonfiction Film*. New York: E. P. Dutton & Company, pp. 232-238 and passim.

Describes the early industrial documentaries (*Meet the Pioneers, Idlers That Work*, and *Three Installations*) as "conventional." The first indications of his later style became evident in *Wakefield Express*, developed in *Thursday's Children*, and culminated in *Every Day Except Christmas. Thursday's Children* forms an important link between "the traditional British documentary and the direct cinema of the 1960s." *Every Day Except Christmas* became "a gentle tribute to the ordinary people who work at uncomplicated tasks."

195. Bates, William. "Social Cinema: Lindsay Anderson." *The Daily California Arts Magazine* (5 July), p. 7.
A brief biographical sketch of Anderson's life and career on the occasion of a retrospective sponsored by the Pacific Film Archive. This was coupled with a showing of *O Lucky Man!*. There is also a short discussion of Anderson's "epic" form which has marked *The White Bus, If...*, and *O Lucky Man!*.

196. Betts, Ernest. *The Film Business: A History of British Cinema 1896-1972*. London: George Allen & Unwin Ltd., pp. 303-306, and passim.
Lindsay Anderson is described as "that rare phenomenon in films, the wholly political animal" and one who addresses himself "exclusively to the social scene." Betts describes Anderson as having found "precisely the style of direction needed for this theme... It was in every way an astonishing performance for a director making his first feature film." He describes *If...* as containing a "more concentrated outburst of hate and destructiveness." The film, a mixture of fantasy and reality, was not intended as a direct attack on the British public school system, but rather as a metaphor for all of British society.

197. Blouin, C. R. Review of *O Lucky Man!. Séquences*, 174 (October), 35-37.
This French review begins by stating that this film is Lindsay Anderson's view of "l'education non-sentimale d'un homme jeune." It proceeds to outline the plot of the movie, singling out McDowell's performance for special notice and comment.

198. Boost, Ch. "Geoprogrammeerd Engagement." *Skoop*, 9 (October), 37.
Mick Travis is described as the synthetic central figure of the film. He is compared to Candide in a general description of the film's plot and Travis' early career. Anderson's style of directing is seen as basically realistic, which is one of the reasons he has gotten into trouble with the critics. Although the film is too long and overloaded with themes, it is reflective and bears Anderson's social/political commentary.

199. Canby, Vincent. "Discussed Any Good Movies?" *The New York Times* (22 July), pp. 1, 8.
Brief notice of *O Lucky Man!* in which he singles out the score for praise, and the screenplay for condemnation (boring). The cast is excellent.

200. Canby, Vincent. "*O Lucky Man!* Ran Out of Luck." *The New York Times* (24 June), section II, pp. 1, 13.
Canby thinks that the film is one of those which is much more interesting to talk about than sit through and that it often winds up "getting reviewed for its intentions instead of its accomplishments." The film sprawls "as if sprawling were a noble end in itself." In fact, the only real continuity is provided by Alan Price's music which also contains the "cool sarcasm and wit that never are fully evident in

the screenplay." Despite the beautiful camera work, the movie fails to achieve its ends; "the content of the satire is either too small or too banal for the form of the film." "Anderson is an intuitive director, yet it's schematicism that inhibits the film, to an even larger extent than it did *If....*"

201. Canby, Vincent. "Screen: 'O Lucky Man!.'" *The New York Times* (14 June), p. 58.

Sees the film as being about literature's classic hero—innocent, wide-eyed and tireless and possessed by such a sweetness of temper that "arbitrary cruelties go unrecognized." The real problem with the film is that Anderson is "much more bold and free as a director than Mr. Sherwin is inventive as a social satirist." The movie always promises to be more than it is. The "wit is too small, too perfunctory, for the grand plan of the film and the quality of the production itself." The three hours become "increasingly nerve-racking." The cast is fine throughout, but the real star of this film for this reviewer is the score by Alan Price. Canby feels that it is the score more than the scenario which carries the satire and bite.

202. Casty, Alan. *Development of the Film.* New York: Harcourt, Brace, Jovanovich, pp. 354-356.

Brief references to both *This Sporting Life* and *If...*, which use the world within the films as a metaphor for the modern world outside the films. With "sharp visual sensitivity and intricacy of editing," Anderson portrays the life of a rugby player by laying the emphasis on the complicity of the rapacious economic system in the destruction of his personal life. *If...* becomes a metaphor for England with its class system, privilege, and outworn traditions. The limits of the film's ironies are difficult to establish, however, because of the breadth of Anderson's satire which encompasses both the rebels and those they are rebelling against.

203. Champlin, Charles. "A Walk on the Vile Side in 'O Lucky Man!'" *Los Angeles Times Calendar* (24 June), pp. 1, 22.

Champlin opens his review by praising Anderson's first two feature films and noting that they were enough to make his reputation as a director of power and individuality. Now with *O Lucky Man!*, Anderson has extended his reputation. Although Anderson remains "cool, guarded, rigorously unsentimental" and thereby detached from his material as well as his audience, he manages to move the viewers of the film to thought and admiration rather more than deep feeling. Anderson is quoted as saying that so few films today leave room for the imagination. In this one, with Anderson providing the cues, the film reveals a "ceaseless power of invention and surprise that is well calculated to hold the audience. The impact is often enormous."

204. Cocks, Jay. "Enlightened Mischief." *Time*, 101 (18 June), 58.

"This nearly overwhelming film is part epic allegory, part lighthearted Brechtian morality play and part three ring circus." Jay Cocks finds *O Lucky Man!* "brash, eclectic, innovative, deeply personal and elusive." He sees the movie as a flashback from the final moment of Zen illumination when Anderson hits McDowell with the rolled up script. The film is complex and provides an ample background for "Anderson's stylistic virtuosity, his sustained energy, his eagerness to explore, to take chances."

205. Coleman, John. "Zen He Go Walkabout." *New Statesman,* 85 (4 May), 666.

Concludes that *O Lucky Man!* is a "lengthier, slacker excursion" than *If*... which "establishes itself a nearly interminable set of straw targets to riddle." Despite the genuinely splendid opening, "funny, exaggerated, wonderfully shot," the movie flags. The film "toys with silent movie techniques ... plays with itself in the back references to Mr. Anderson's small canon of product," and it is both arrogant and anarchistic. "It is very open to the sort of exegesis that ambitious snails were built to undertake."

206. Cowie, Peter, ed. *International Film Guide, 1973.* New York: A. S. Barnes & Co., p. 159.

Brief mention of the credits for *O Lucky Man!*.

207. Delmas, Jean. "Le Meilleur des Mondes." *Jeune Cinema,* 74 (November), 44-47.

Following a synopsis of the plot of *O Lucky Man!* during which the reviewer discusses the film's epic quality, he talks about the genesis of the idea from McDowell's story. He also compares the film with Kubrick's *Clockwork Orange* and the later films of Andrzej Munk, the Polish director.

208. Duffy, Martha. "An Ethic of Work and Play." *Sports Illustrated,* 38 (5 March), 66-74, 77-78, 80-81.

An account of David Storey's play *The Changing Room* in which Storey relates something of what went into the composition of his script. Brief mention of Lindsay Anderson as the director of the play.

209. Flatley, Guy. "Anderson: 'We have to make our own acts of courage.'" *The New York Times* (1 July), section II, pp. 1, 17.

Chatty interview with Anderson who was in the United States to promote *O Lucky Man!*. The piece contains some biographical information, Anderson's ideas on his films, and his reactions to some of the criticism leveled at them. Anderson's reaction to Pauline Kael is especially quotable: "[she] is such a caricature of the journalistic bitch." Also mentions some of the early documentaries and Anderson's stint as a critic on *Sequence,* "one of those vitriolic little magazines people run when they are young."

210. Freund, Klas and Lars-Olaf Löthwall. "The Anderson Tape." Translated by Klas Freund. *Chaplin,* 124: 174-175.

In this interview at the Cannes Film Festival, Anderson discusses a number of films, film styles, directors, and his reaction to critics and his own films. Apparently there was a near scandal at the festival when Anderson accused the French press of asking only idiotic questions and providing nonchalant appraisals of *O Lucky Man!*. The rest of the interview deals with Anderson's comments about other directors such as Bergman, Fellini, and Godard. He discusses the general theme of his own films which deal with a contemporary social malaise. Anderson thinks of his films as a truly popular art form.

211. Gertner, Richard. *International Motion Picture Almanac, 1973.* New York: Quigley Publishing Company, p. 6.

Lists Anderson's major documentary films, the Robin Hood television series, feature films, and theater productions through 1973. Includes credits for artistic director at the Royal Court (1969-1970), contributing editor of *Sequence*, Anderson's association with the Free Cinema group and National Film Theatre (1956-1959), and awards for *Thursday's Children* and *Every Day Except Christmas*. Also a brief biography.

212. Hatch, Robert. Review of *O Lucky Man!*. *Nation*, 217 (2 July), 27-28.

The major problem with this film for this reviewer is the theme: "that success, like happiness, is not a goal but a by-product of life." He finds the idea banal and the film bogged down by an unoriginal script which tries to compensate for the lack by "inventing grotesque, ludicrous and horrifying ways" of dealing with the evils of our time. "What it comes down to is that *O Lucky Man!* aspires to be a serious denunciation of present evils but comes across as an entertainment based on clichés of social criticism."

213. Head, Anne. "Lindsay Anderson et *O Lucky Man!*: echos de tournage." *Revue du Cinema/Image et Son*, 272 (May), 85-89.

A review of *O Lucky Man!* which incorporates portions of an interview with Anderson. The reviewer singles out the music and the acting for special comment, and notes that Anderson has a unique position as a British filmmaker since he seems to be able to attract American financial help for his projects, even though these projects remain staunchly British in subject matter.

214. Hepnerova, Eva. "Rekli v Cannis: Lindsay Anderson." *Film a Doba*, 19 (August), 403-432.

The article begins by pointing out the connections between *O Lucky Man!* and *Candide*, but also points out the differences in subtleties. This reviewer describes the film as a "collective dilemma," even though there is much talent in the film. The author does not agree with the film's analogies with Brecht. The critic sees closer alliances with Buñuel's *Viridiana*. The film is also compared to Stanley Kubrick's *A Clockwork Orange*, but where Kubrick attempts to reach a spiritual depth, Anderson satirizes it.

215. Hudson, Christopher. "Christopher Hudson on Something to Smile About." *The Spectator*, No. 7559 (12 May), 595-596.

"*O Lucky Man!* is a funny, bawdy, exhilarating slapdash piece of cinema which should be seen by everybody over the age of consent and under the age of placid acceptance." It is, however, "overlong, diffuse, over-ambitious," but he feels that more British directors should overreach themselves. Despite Anderson's intentions, his shift of perspective confuses the audience and loses much of the satiric bite of the film. "'I am not a cynic,'" Anderson is quoted as saying; " 'only sentimentalists talk about cynicism.'" But it left the reviewer wondering what he does think about the world.

216. Jensen, Niels. "Lindsay Anderson—Romantisk Ironiker." *Kosmorama*, 20 (November), 43-53.

A long formal essay on Anderson, including materials about his biography, film work, scenarios, and credits. Also an analysis of his style, his point of view, and his film philosophy.

217. Kael, Pauline. "Smile and Say 'Spinach.'"*The New Yorker*, 49 (16 June), 80, 82-83.

 Pauline Kael describes *O Lucky Man!* as "Anderson's most complex, irascible, and contenting feature so far." A mixture of "rebelliousness, Socratic questioning, and affection," the film has a fine script with a vein for the vernacular and a clear eye for hypocrisy. "The director's reverence for simplicities comes through like a clarion," and it reflects an interesting Brechtian morality revealing as it does Brecht's "peculiar mixture of formalism and charity."

218. Kauffmann, Stanley. Review of *O Lucky Man!*. *New Republic*, 168 (16 June), 24, 33.

 "For a decade or so, there was promise that Lindsay Anderson might become a British analogue of Ingmar Bergman—a good theater director who went to films as a place where he could be creator more than interpreter." Now Kauffmann doesn't think this is possible. "The film exudes conceit and pigheadedness, is steeped in self-display and self-reference, a three-hour effort at self-canonization." In spite of the good direction, the film is only a "laborious sophomoric dud." Of the final scene where Anderson strikes Malcolm McDowell in order to get him to smile, Kauffmann says, "I had the feeling that the very long, heavily fraught enterprise had been created for just that blow, so Anderson could strike someone else on screen, an actor, a creation of his, like a master, like a thaumaturge, like a demigod ordaining life." It revolted him: "It was the single most sickening, self-indulgent, ego-drooling moment I've seen on film...." Finally, he feels that Anderson has nothing to say and that out of "this mess of pretentiousness and egotism and aimless skill" a great zero emerges. "A great zero for this film and a hovering zero for Anderson's film future."

219. Lajeunasse, J. "Le Meilleur des Mondes Possibles." *Revue du Cinema/Image et Son*, No. 276/277 (October), 242-243.

 A brief notice of *O Lucky Man!* which lists the credits, a succinct resume, and a short critique. The direction is brilliant.

220. Landau, Jon. "Films: Mazursky on love, lawyers, shrinks, and chic radicals." *Rolling Stone*, 141 (16 August), 58-59.

 O Lucky Man! is riddled, for this reviewer, by "pretension, calculation, and a cold English intellectuality," and it lacks the clarity of *If . . .* which compensated for the "directorial frostiness and distant point of view" of that earlier film. He also finds the film overly long; for him only three individual sections actually work (about 30 minutes of the movie). He suggests cutting the film drastically even though it "wouldn't have said any less to this view than it does in its current flabby state."

221. Lefeure, Raymond. "Le Meilleur des Mondes Possible." *Cinema*, 73, no. 182 (December), 148-149.

 A short notice of *O Lucky Man!* in which Mick's travels are compared with Candide's, travels which are fraught with terror and venom. The film gives the audience an ironic look at modern society on a par with Kafka.

222. MacCann, Richard Dyer. *The People's Films*. New York: Hastings House, pp. 29, 31.

 Mentions Anderson's essay "Only Connect" (*see* no. 388) and the Free Cinema films: *Thursday's Children, O Dreamland, Every Day Except Christmas.* Anderson is also cited as a critic for *Sight and Sound* and *Sequence*; he was "not a Grierson man. They did not linger long in the documentary pulpit."

223. Magill, Marcia. Review of *O Lucky Man!*. *Films in Review*, 24 (August/September), 434-435.

O Lucky Man! is a three hour morality play, but one in which the time passes swiftly and entertainingly. In spite of the fact that the film is about the corruption of the establishment, the film is "often witty and imaginative, told with a thumb to the nose and a tongue to the cheek, always on the fringe of tumbling over into the absurd but always controlled."

224. Manchel, Frank. *Film-Study—A Resource Guide.* Cranbury, N.J.: Associated University Presses, pp. 290-291 and passim.

Several short sources of information about Anderson, including a brief synopsis of *If...,* a "splendid film," and an evaluation of Elizabeth Sussex's book on the filmmaker, a "rather shallow text."

225. Michalek, Boleslaw. Review of *O Lucky Man!*. *Kino*, 8 (December), 58-59.

A lengthy review of *O Lucky Man!,* this article begins by introducing Malcolm McDowell, listing his films and so on. His central role in the film is compared to that in *Candide,* and the film is described as demystifying, humorous, ironic. After a brief discussion of Anderson's career as a documentary-realist and pioneer in the Free Cinema movement, the critic summarizes the basic political and social themes of his films, generalizing on their impact in the history of film. Finally, the article includes a rather detailed delineation of the plot and concludes by comparing the film to Kubrick's *A Clockwork Orange.* The critic declares that the film is Anderson's most mature and reflective.

226. Milne, Tom. Review of *O Lucky Man! Monthly Film Bulletin*, 40, no. 473 (June), 128-129.

The film has some flaws largely, thinks this reviewer, because Anderson is more "interested in getting at the system than in exploring his central character." He finds a certain charm in the "picaresque aspect of Mick's pilgrim's progress," but the film finally succumbs to self-indulgence. "Anderson's record has got stuck—despite the debatable Zen—about ten years back with the old humanist cry of despair about them and us," a cry which is badly undercut by the "pretentious paraphenalia of borrowings (including Fellini, no less), in-jokes and self-justification."

227. Oakes, Philip, ed. "Coming On: Getting the Right Price." *Sunday Times* (London) (22 April), p. 37.

News item about Alan Price who took two years to write the score for *O Lucky Man!.* Apparently he was terrified of appearing in the film and admits to getting through the filming sessions on "Newcastle Brown and most of us got thoroughly puddled." He was preparing to travel to Cannes to promote the film which was the official entry of Great Britain in 1973.

228. Pechter, W. S. "Politics on Film." *Commentary,* 56 (September), 74-77.

Pechter feels that the film is a failure on several counts. First, the irony which is supposed to pervade the atmosphere of the film doesn't always come off. Second, much of the satire is sophomoric. Finally, although Anderson regards the work as subversive, Pechter sees it as "decidedly half-hearted, and weighed down by a terrible complacency of spirit."

229. Putterman, Barry. "A Lost and Found Weekend." *Audience*, 6 (July), 7.
A rather breezy account of the Warner Brothers weekend at Yale University for the press representatives assigned to cover the opening of *O Lucky Man!*. Unfortunately, this reviewer found the movie a clinker. Overdone and derivative, the movie turned out "to be just another sophomoric pseudo-satire debunking the same old overused targets."

230. Rothenbuecher, B. "Not Yet a Man." *Christian Century*, 90 (15-22 August), 809-810.
"*O Lucky Man!* is a disappointment—because it could have been a great movie and it isn't." So begins this review in which the author faults Anderson for creating a mid-twentieth century *Jederman* but without allowing us to identify with him. She feels that whatever exhilaration we might feel while watching the film stems from the smooth technical proficiency of the acting, editing, direction, and photography. The music, both vital and original, provides the film with some continuity. But the audience does not feel any connection, "intense emotional reaction" or "gut-wrenching" identification with the hero. "In this odyssey Anderson fails to communicate his own point of view." So his film ends up as soft as his protagonist.

231. Sherwin, David. "Dagbok Med Ett Manus." Translated by K. Freund. *Chaplin*, 124, 171-173.
A lighthearted, almost flippant description of the production of *O Lucky Man!* in a journal format. Various meetings between McDowell and Anderson in various places are listed by date. The article describes the daily life of an artist and the conversations which went on about casting, titles, production, and so on.

232. Sherwin, David. "Diary of a Script," in *O Lucky Man!* by Lindsay Anderson and David Sherwin with songs by Alan Price. New York: Grove Press, pp. 10-22.
A rather detailed account in diary form of the genesis and development of the script. Sherwin mentions Anderson's impatience and the various starts and stops the script experienced. Interspersed in the diary entries are asides about what the other principals in the film are doing: Anderson, Price, and McDowell. Sherwin also includes some rather interesting material on the origin of various scenes in the film (*see* no. 231).

233. Walsh, Moira. Review of *O Lucky Man! America*, 129 (7 July), 20.
In spite of the savagely funny individual moments of black comedy, the first-rate camera work, the rock score, and the supporting cast, the film fails, because "at its center the film has pretentious delusions of social satire, whereas its viewpoint seldom rises above the level of the banal and sophomoric iconoclasm."

234. Westerbeck, Colin L. Jr. "The Spider's Stratagem." *Commonweal*, 98 (21 September), 501-502.
Westerbeck notes that it has been five years since Anderson's last feature film *If...*, and that the length of time has obviously put a strain on *O Lucky Man!* by making it carry too much weight. "Perhaps if he would work a bit faster than a

film every five years, Anderson wouldn't fall into these mix-ups between figment and fact. It might take a great load off his mind were he able to think of his imagination as having less consequence." The reviewer is dissatisfied with the film and what he perceives as Anderson's arrogance in assuming that the film could right the topsy-turvy world depicted in it. "Can Anderson really think that his making a film about the ills of the world will cure them, or at least compensate us who suffer them?" He leaves the last question unanswered.

235. Williams, J. Peter. "Movie Mailbag: What Wit?" *The New York Times* (5 August), section II, p. 4.

A letter to the editor criticizing Loraine Alterman's review of *O Lucky Man!* in the *New York Times* (*see* no. 184). Mr Williams feels that to judge a film by its plot would pay it the same injustice as judging a song solely on the basis of its lyrics.

236. Wilson, David. Review of *O Lucky Man!*. *Sight and Sound*, 42, no. 3 (Summer), 126-129.

Beginning with a quotation from Anderson's 1957 article "Get Out and Push!" (*see* no. 421) to the effect that Britain was mired in a stultifying mediocrity, philistinism, and smugness, David Wilson explores *O Lucky Man!* in search of Anderson's current direction. The film, built on epic proportions, deals with the central character's journey "from illusion to a smiling acceptance of reality." The epic form of the film allows Anderson to hedge a bit on his criticism of contemporary society: "the epic form is a convenient vehicle for the non-specific, for rounded synthesis rather than pointed analysis." Rather than the "easy generalities of an epic panorama," the reviewer wishes Anderson would clarify the nature of his beliefs.

237. Wooten, James T. "Capital Film Festival Opens to Dispute." *The New York Times* (4 April), p. 34.

Mentions that Lindsay Anderson had withdrawn *O Lucky Man!* in protest against the American Film Institute's refusal to play Costa-Gavras' film, *State of Siege,* during the institute's inaugural season in the new theater. A number of directors had withdrawn films to be shown during the opening season of the theater.

238. Z[immerman], P[aul] D. "Mick on the Make." *Newsweek*, 81 (25 June), 55.

With *O Lucky Man!* Lindsay Anderson has made a complete conversion to fantasy. Like Stanley Kubrick, Anderson has found "realism an increasingly inadequate mode for tackling the truths of modern life." But his "sharp satiric eye gives his fantasy a firm anchor to social reality." It is only when Anderson moves to examine social corruption that his narrow "Marxist perspective cuts the moral complexities out of his theme and characters, reducing them to clichés." It is only when Anderson draws from life itself that his film works, and not from the "simplistic left-wing ideas that elsewhere make this film as obvious as it is ambitious."

1974

239. Bobker, Lee R. *Elements of Film.* Second edition. New York: Harcourt, Brace and World, Inc., pp.105, 128.

O Lucky Man! is mentioned as an example of how a sound track can alternate between "direct and indirect relationships to the film images." He briefly discusses Alan Price's music which not only provides underscoring for the visual images but counterpoint as well. And the lyrics bridge the various sections of the film. Bobker also singles out *This Sporting Life* for the impact of editing used by Anderson to involve the audience in the brutality of the rugby scenes.

240. Burch, Noel. "Four French Documentaries," in *The Documentary Tradition: From Nanook to Woodstock.* Selected, arranged and introduced by Lewis Jacobs. New York: Hopkinson and Blake, pp. 318-326.
Reprint of no. 52.

241. Cowie, Peter. Review of *O Lucky Man!,* in *International Film Guide, 1974.* New York: A. S. Barnes & Company, pp. 135, 138.
"With irony as pungent as Swift's, and with moments of vision that commemorate Blake or Chaplin, Lindsay Anderson's *O Lucky Man!* fulfills all the promise of his earlier work, and demonstrates that he is still the only indigenous English director of real stature." He finds the film "a vigorous denunciation of the materialistic society" which, despite its length, is not overly long because of Anderson's eye for detail, for his provincial English mannerisms, and for the shabby geography of the urban north.

242. Cunningham, Frank R. "Lindsay Anderson's *O Lucky Man!* and the Romantic Tradition." *Literature/Film Quarterly,* 2, no. 3 (Summer), 256-261.
Cunningham perceives the film as "a major work of the imagination, visually compelling, thematically deep, and philosophically courageous ... a rich example of the tradition of literary and cinematic Romanticism." This reviewer finds the central character of the film undergoing the traditional romantic change of character, from "absorption in self or in self-defeating abstractions to the discovery of a universe far greater than his initial conceptions of it." Mick goes from a state of "joyless ambition" to a reunification with the life forces in the universe by making a moral choice and thereby defining his reality and shaping it to his needs.

243. Durgnat, Raymond. *"O Lucky Man!* or: the Adventures of a Clockwork Cheese." *Film Comment,* 10 (January/February), 38-40.
In this impressionistic review, Durgnat throws together a pastiche of film titles, pop songs, references to other motion pictures (some of them referred to in the film), and allusions to Anderson's other movies and comes up with a composite view of the film as a product of the British of the early 70s.

244. Gertner, Richard, ed. *International Motion Picture Almanac, 1974.* New York: Quigley Publishing Company, p. 6.
Encyclopedic entry similar to that in the 1973 edition.

245. Jacobs, Lewis. "New Trends in British Documentary: Free Cinema," in *The Documentary Tradition: From Nanook to Woodstock.* Selected, arranged and introduced by Lewis Jacobs. New York: Hopkinson and Blake, pp. 334-338.
Reprint of no. 51.

246. Jacobs, Lewis. "The Turn Towards Conservatism," in *The Documentary Tradition: From Nanook to Woodstock*. Selected, arranged and introduced by Lewis Jacobs. New York: Hopkinson and Blake, pp. 276-282.

Brief mention of *Thursday's Children, O Dreamland,* and *Every Day Except Christmas* as nonconformist documentaries whose focus "fell more sharply upon the harsher realities of the modern world." These and other films like them became the foundation for the Free Cinema movement.

247. Marszalek, Rafal. "Lindsay Anderson." *Kino,* 9 (October), 41-48.

The article begins with a filmography and a generalization about Anderson's status as one of the world's foremost filmmakers. Notes his award for *If...* and his connection with the Free Cinema movement. What follows is an analysis of Anderson's films stressing their socio-political content. For example, he sees *If...* as primarily a critique of "old England," its political system in particular. All of this helps to define Anderson's view of reality. The critic sees Anderson as a rebel against a rigid and unthinking system: "Stupid thinking breeds stupid consequences." Finally the author concludes that Anderson's films posit a dialectic between analytical thought and synthetic thinking, between observation and creation, between the obvious and the intuitive. Anderson uses a form of the fable to develop a documentary.

248. Michael, Joseph. "Book Reviews: 'Hollywood, England: The British Film Industry in the Sixties,' by Alexander Walker." *Sight and Sound,* 43, no. 4 (Autumn), 249-250.

The book sets up two creative periods in British cinema, the Forties and the Sixties. Anderson is cited as one of those who worked in Britain in the Sixties and was an advocate of "provincial realism" with *This Sporting Life.* Walker also mentions the symbolic use of violence in British films of the period, citing *If...* and the slap at the end of *O Lucky Man!* as two examples.

249. Millar, Jeff. Review of *O Lucky Man!. Film Heritage,* 9, no. 4 (Summer), 36-37.

"Instead of an important film passing through in the guise of a trifle—the traditional source for aesthetes prospecting for masterpieces—*Man* seems to be a trifle cunningly, impishly disguised as a masterpiece." The reviewer sees the entire film as a satire, even the pretentiousness, "the appearance of pretension, of weight and mysterious literary resonance, is one of its comedic devices." Although the film is "some intellectual's idle exercise designed for the casual entertainment of the uselessly educated," it is nevertheless enjoyable partly because of these very qualities. As long as one does not take the film seriously but rather plays the game along with Anderson, it is all great fun and a fascinating experience.

250. Oakes, Philip, ed. "Coming On: Britical." *Sunday Times* (London) (9 June), p. 37.

Mentions that Anderson is going to film David Storey's play "In Celebration" for the distinguished series, American Film Theater. On being told that the series had not yet played in Britain, Anderson remarked, "I have a very low opinion of the British film industry *and* the British public." He believes that the films should get the widest possible distribution in England, but on this occasion he wouldn't mind giving Great Britain a miss altogether.

251. Rumalho, Jose Jorge. "Un Filme que Evoca Jean Vigo." *Celuloide,* 17 (November), 29-30.

This review of *If...* begins with a brief biography of Anderson and his socio-political views. After a short description of the plot of the film, the article discusses the English educational system which was the basis of Anderson's focus. The reviewer compares the microcosm of the school with a traditional, conservative, Western capitalist system. *If...* is also compared to Vigo's *Zero for Conduct* in that they both use a Brechtian dramaturgy and concern themselves with themes of actuality.

252. Schever, Steven. *The Movie Book.* Chicago: The Ridge Press/Playboy Press, p. 79.

Mentions *This Sporting Life* as one of those films which helped to "create a new vision of working-class England."

253. Taylor, John Russell. "Tomorrow the World: Some Reflections on the Un-Englishness of English Films." *Sight and Sound,* 43, no. 2 (Spring), 80-83.

Taylor discusses the interrelations between the American and British film worlds, especially with the devalued pound. He mentions that British films do not always pay their way in America and mentions *O Lucky Man!* as a case in point. He also questions Anderson's right to be called a director of "international" reputation. Certainly the "intensity of vision and dazzling gifts of self-expression" make accessible the British way of life to a wider audience, but does that make him an international filmmaker?

254. Wilson, David. "Images of Britain." *Sight and Sound,* 43, no. 2 (Spring), 85-86.

Brief mention of *This Sporting Life* as one of those films which was hailed at the time as "ushering a new and vital era of British cinema." It is the "only major British film of the early Sixties which hasn't dated."

255. Winogura, D. Review of *O Lucky Man! Cinafantastique,* 3, no. 2, 28

This review begins by saying that *O Lucky Man!* is one "of the most original and unparalleled fantasy odysseys in the history of the cinema." This film is Anderson's "bold, complex masterpiece," and is his "liveliest, clear-lined, and most compelling achievement to date." The reviewer compares the film with Swift or Carroll or Voltaire, one with a style brilliant and under control. The film is an important cornerstone in modern cinema.

256. Wright, Basil. *The Long View.* London: Secker and Warburg, pp. 547-548 and passim.

Brief references to the Free Cinema movement, Anderson's article about *On the Waterfront (see* no. 403), and Anderson's help and advice in editing Lester James Peries' film, *Rekava.* There is also a discussion of Anderson's later commercial work: *This Sporting Life, The White Bus, If...,* and *The Singing Lesson.*

1975

257. Canby, Vincent. "Storey's 'In Celebration' Is Moving Film." *The New York Times* (18 March), p. 30.

After praising the play and the performances of the actors, Canby praises Anderson for "making a very complete full-bodied film of Mr. Storey's play without being tricky or intrusive.... When the camera ranges beyond the Shaw parlor, the principal battleground, there is always a point to the movement."

258. Cocks, Jay. "Dead Center." *Time,* 105 (17 February), 4.

"This was David Storey's second play, written before he had fully found and measured the silences." The play is a highly personal one for Storey and the film uses the original cast from the Royal Court production with great skill. "Under Anderson's direction, the movie gathers enormous force, partly from the raw skill of its actors, partly from the accumulating tension of frustration." The director's "skill cannot make the play any more complete or successful, but it does make it happen superbly well."

259. Crist, Judith. Review of *In Celebration. New York Magazine,* 8 (17 March), 77.

In 1975 Crist thought that this film was "one of the finest American Film Theater offerings to date," and that Anderson had "shown such sensitivity and perception in the filming of the drama, in barely opening the sets but doing so with an intensity of atmosphere that was overwhelming." The film quite simply "offers the best of film and filmed theatre."

260. Gertner, Richard, ed. *International Motion Picture Almanac, 1975.* New York: Quigley Publishing Company, p. 5.

Encyclopedic entry similar to that of 1973, plus a reference to *In Celebration.*

261. Gomez, Joseph A. "British Documentary: Grierson, Jennings and Free Cinema." *Literature/Film Quarterly,* 3 (Winter), 91-92.

This review of *Studies in Documentary* by Alan Lovell and Jim Hillier notes that "the attitudes of the Free Cinema tradition have meaning today only through the works of Anderson." Brief mention of *O Lucky Man!* as having sense if looked at from the perspective of the Free Cinema aesthetic.

262. Haskell, Molly. "The Truth Game." *Village Voice,* 20 (31 March), 76-77.

Reviewer Haskell describes the play film as "that category of middle-class domestic drama that has by now taken on the familiar lineaments of a genre." Anderson takes this rather cliché plot and makes something new out of it. Fully at home with the excellent cast and thoroughly familiar with Storey's drama—Anderson has directed most if not all of his plays—Anderson uses a minimum of cutting and editing, thereby heightening those effects when he does use film techniques for emphasis.

263. Kauffmann, Stanley. *Living Images: Film Comment and Criticism.* New York: Harper & Row, pp. 204-207 and passim.

Reprints his review of *O Lucky Man!* (*see* no. 218). He also makes several passing criticisms of *If...*, for example, that it is derivative and that there are several stylistic idiosyncracies in the film which make no sense.

264. Lovell, Alan. "Brecht in Britain—Lindsay Anderson." *Screen,* 16, no. 4 (Winter), pp. 62-80.

The purpose of this article is to condense the proceedings of a discussion on

"Film and Politics" which centered on the Brechtian elements in Anderson's films *If . . .* and *O Lucky Man!.* The discussion's central question focused on the tensions a socialist filmmaker like Anderson faces trying to work within the capitalist cinema world, making films which convey information to a mass audience while entertaining them, and at the same time dealing with avant-garde elements of the film which might be personally engaging but distancing to that mass audience. Anderson, not wanting to be simply conformist, has skirted the problem. There follows a discussion of the ways in which *If . . .* and *O Lucky Man!* either do or do not fit into a Brechtian mold.

265. McCreadie, Marsha. Review of *In Celebration. Films in Review,* 26 (May), 313-314.

In Celebration will hold you in its grip and wipe you out "as only a family reunion can." The cast is brilliantly led by Alan Bates. "Within its British framework the complexity of family life, with its combinations of love, hope, obligation, memory and resentment, is brilliantly realized."

266. Tads (J.P. Tadros). Review of *In Celebration. Variety,* 277 (22 January), 35.

This reviewer thinks that the play has been highly successfully adapted to the screen, largely because of the long association between Anderson and the actors and between Anderson and David Storey, the writer. The story, so "intense and emotional, needs the tightknit understanding, not to say complicity, which these actors and their director have been able to build." Finds this film an "important documenting of modern theatre."

267. Taylor, John R. "Lindsay Anderson," in *Directors and Directions.* New York: Hill and Wang, pp. 68-99.

A lengthy article surveying both Anderson's life and his work. Taylor describes Anderson as the only director presently working in Britain who can call himself an international figure, "who can without apology or special pleading be considered in the same frame of reference as Pasolini or Jansco or Ray—who is, in short, undoubtedly and unarguably an *auteur.*" A director with "considerable technical abilities," he is also a man with a complex temperament, with a "burning necessity to express himself in film" which he does with a recognizable style and message.

1976

268. Bawden, Liz-Anne, ed. *The Oxford Companion to Film.* New York: Oxford University Press, pp. 17-18.

General account of Anderson's work and career as a film critic and filmmaker. His "clarity and determination about his aims as a critic and practicing filmmaker have made him more influential than any other single figure in unsettling the complacency of the British film industry."

269. Brown, Geoff. Review of *In Celebration. Monthly Film Bulletin,* 43, no. 506 (March), pp. 54-55.

A brief synopsis of the play with credits plus a short résumé of what changes Storey made in the play for the screen adaption. The play is dealing with familiar material, a north of England miner who is married to a woman above him socially, but despite this, it does have a "cumulative power largely because of Anderson's theatre background. Anderson trains his camera on the actors with a theatre director's concern for the overall balance of a scene and the careful interaction of its motley participants."

270. Cameron, Ian. "Family Plots." *Spectator,* 236 (19 June), 28-29.
Brief mention of *In Celebration* as a superior piece of work. Anderson's great self-restraint with the camerawork focused attention on the actors.

271. Coleman, John "Wizard of Oz." *New Statesman,* 91 (11 June), 790-791.
Very brief mention of *In Celebration.* Marvelous redoing of the stage play. "One wishes his stoic, anarchic entries into world cinema had had as much style."

272. Durgnat, Raymond. "Brittania Waives the Rules." *Film Comment,* 12 (July-August), 50-59.
Anderson is discussed in the context of current British filmmakers as one of the "triumvirate" of talents who went beyond mere "leftist or liberal reformers or even a particular generation" in their films (the other two were Tony Richardson and Karel Reisz). *This Sporting Life* is described as going beyond the "lyrical but two-dimensional portraiture of the working classes in the Free Cinema films" into a profounder ambivalence. *If...* violated all conceptions of the public school subgenre of movies in favor of a romantic fantasy. *O Lucky Man!* turned the theme of "hard-edged ambition into a full-blown satire on British life." Both anger and irony were successfully combined in the film.

273. Rhode, Eric. *A History of the Cinema from its Origins to 1970.* London: Alan Lane-Penguin, pp. 543, 606, 609.
Brief references to *If...,* Anderson's activity in the Free Cinema movement, and *This Sporting Life.*

274. Thomson, David. *A Biographical Dictionary of Film.* New York: William Morrow and Company, Inc., pp. 5-6.
Anderson is mentioned as one of the "more active and idiosyncratic figures in the British arts." Unfortunately, his "contradictoriness" will be "vigorous enough to prevent him from a filmmaking career that has any continuity." The critic feels that Anderson's "energies are unresolved and that his rather prickly talent has never been fully expressed." The author liked *If...* ("what a film for a young man to have made") and disliked *O Lucky Man!,* "something an older man will hope to forget."

1977

275. Anon. Review of Lindsay Anderson. The *Times* (London) (6 February), p. 17.
Anderson is described as fulfilling "the Continental definition of the director as a man who is something of a philosopher, or guru, as well as an interpreter of plays." Anderson is the custodian of certain values, many of which are associated with the working class in the north of England.

276. Kauffmann, Stanley. "A Cost of Freedom." *The New Republic,* 177 (1 October), 26-28.
In this essay on the function of the film director, Kauffmann discusses the

disappointment of a real directing talent being ruined by his insistence that he control the entire film. The case in point, the one Kauffmann always thinks of first, is Lindsay Anderson. Kauffmann sees Anderson as a highly talented director who has trouble with form. Of the four major films, however, Kauffmann feels that *In Celebration* is the best because Anderson was bound by the script and thereby was given a form for the film.

277. Monaco, James. *How to Read a Film: The Art, Technology, Language, History, and Theory of Film and Media.* New York: Oxford University Press, p. 268.

Single mention of Anderson as the "most ambitious director" of the young British directors who emerged during the late 50s and early 60s.

Performances, Writings, and Other Film Related Activity

FILM & THEATRE RELATED ACTIVITY

278.	1952	*The Pleasure Garden* by James Broughton: Production manager.
279.	1953	*Together* by Lorenza Mazzetti: Supervising editor.
280.	1958	*March to Aldermaston* by an 11-member committee, including Anderson, which produced and directed the film: Supervising editor.
281.	1959	*Rekava (The Line of Life)* by Lester James Peries: Editorial assistance.
282.	1959-1960	Royal Court Theatre: Associate director.
283.	1960	*The Lily White Boys* by Harry Cookson: filmed insert.
284.	1964-1965	Royal Court Theatre: Artistic director.
285.	1969-1970	British Film Institute: Member of the board of governors.

PERFORMANCES IN FILM & THEATRE

286.	1952	*The Pleasure Garden* by James Broughton: small part.
287.	1955	*Henry* by Lindsay Anderson: NSPCC officer.
288.	1967	*The Parachute* by David Mercer, directed by Anthony Page: Gestapo-lawyer.
289.	1968	*Inadmissible Evidence* by John Osborne, directed by Anthony Page: Barrister.
290.	1973	*O Lucky Man!* by Lindsay Anderson; himself.

AWARDS

291.	1953	*Thursday's Children*: Hollywood Academy, Best Short Subject.
292.	1957	*Every Day Except Christmas*: Grand Prix Venice International Film Festival, Best Documentary.

293.	1963	*This Sporting Life*: Cannes International Film Festival, Official British entry; Richard Harris: Best Actor, Rachel Roberts: Best Actress.
294.	1964	British Film Academy Awards. Best Actress: Rachel Roberts. Nominated Best Actor: Richard Harris. Academy of Motion Picure Arts and Sciences. Nominated Best Actor: Richard Harris. Nominated Best Supporting Actress: Rachel Roberts.
295.	1968	"Fat Chef" (commercial for Alcan): Gold Award, American Commercial TV Festival.
296.	1969	*If...*: Grand Prix Cannes International Film Festival, Best Film.
297.	1969	*T.V. Mail*: Director of the Year.
298.	1970	*International Film Guide*: Director of the Year.

TELEVISION FILMS

Episodes in *The Adventures of Robin Hood* series. Incorporated Television Programme Company (Weinstein Productions for Sapphire Films). Directed by Lindsay Anderson. Executive producer: Hannah Weinstein. Associate producer: Sidney Cole. Script supervisor: Albert G. Ruben. Photographed by Ken Hodges. Supervising editor: Thelma Connell. Art supervisor: William Kellner. Sound: H.C. Pearson. Assistant director: Christopher Noble. Production manager: Harold Buck. Each 25 minutes.

299.	1955	*Secret Mission*. Screenplay by Ralph Smart. Music by Edwin Astley.
300.	1956	*The Imposters*. Screenplay by Norman Best. Music by Edwin Astley.
301.	1956	*Ambush*. Screenplay by Ernest Borneman and Ralph Smart. Music by Albert Elms.
302.	1956	*The Haunted Mill*. Screenplay by Paul Symonds. Music by Edwin Astley.
303.	1956	*Isabella*. Screenplay by Neil R. Collins. Music by Edwin Astley.
		Actors: Richard Greene, Bernadette O'Farrell, Alan Wheatley, Alexander Gauge, John Dearth, and Peter Bennett.

TELEVISION COMMERCIALS

304.	1963	MACKESON
		Cameraman: Larry Pizer. With Bernard Miles.
		"You have what you like."
		"I'm not telling you to drink Mackeson."
		"Consider for a moment."
		"Just think of Mackeson."

"Switch off and slip out for a Mackeson."
"This chap has been shovelling snow."
"If you are longing for something."
"If there was a knock at your door."
"Old King Charles."
"Mackeson, what a lovely word."
"Worried about your night's sleep?"
"Old Fred King—he was the father of triplets."
"I wish I had nothing else to do all day."
"Ned Dyson fell off the church steeple."
"You'll learn as you grow older."
"If you're all on your own."
"Nothing to be ashamed of, you know."
(September)

305. 1963 *PERSIL*
Cameraman: Gerry Turpin.
"Raglan in Dover."
(September)

306. 1963 *FRY'S PICNIC*
Cameraman: Larry Pizer. With Tony Wall, Roy Coombes, Blanche Moore.
"Factory."
(October)

307. 1963 *FRY'S PICNIC*
Cameraman: Larry Pizer. With Ray Smith, Harry Goodyear, Stanley Dupree.
"Woodsman"
(November)

308. 1963 *ROWNTREE*
Cameraman: Larry Pizer.
"Barber Shop"
"Fringe"
"Shoe Shop"
"Launderette"
"Model Cars"
"Photograph"
(November)

309. 1964 *ROWNTREE*
Cameraman: Larry Pizer.
"Train"
"Museum"
"Cinema"
"Hat Shop"
(June)

310. 1964   *HORLICKS*
Cameraman: Gerry Turpin.
"Kite 1"
"Kite 11"
(August)

311. 1964   *MACKESON*
Cameraman: Larry Pizer. With Bernard Miles.
"Water.... you can't beat it."
"Gran Hardy was saying"
"Old Gran Hardy" (alternative)
"Now any young couple"
"When the long days behind"
"Old Joe Sturgess"
"When you've had a row with the Missus"
"When I'm driving"
"When you get the kids to bed"
"When you're odds on favourite"(Winter)
"When you're odds on favourite" (Summer)
"There's no doubt at all."
"Trade Shot"
(October)

312. 1965   *RONSON RAZOR*
Cameraman: A. Thompson. With Mollie Neville.
"Barber 1"
"Barber 2"
(May)

313. 1965   *MACKESON*
Cameraman: Larry Pizer. With Bernard Miles, Hilda
Fenmore.
"She does what she's told."
"Come on, say Mackeson." (parrot)
"Take good care."
"Grasp the friendly Mackeson bottle."
"That looks good, tastes good."
"One sure draw that never lets you down."
"My old dad reckoned"
(December)

314. 1965   *WHITBREAD TANKARD*
Cameraman: Larry Pizer. With Bernard Warner, Jack
Waters.
"Rowing"
Cameraman: Larry Pizer. With Rugby Club Players.
"Rugby"
(December)

315. 1967   *ALCAN*
                  Cameraman: Norman Warwick. With John Sharpe.
                  "Fat Chef"
                  (September)

316. 1968   *BLACK MAGIC*
                  Cameraman: Larry Pizer. With Bridgette Brice.
                  "Taxi"
                  (November)

317. 1968   *KRAFT C/B*
                  Cameraman: Larry Pizer. With James Robertson
                  Justice.
                  "Silver Paper"
                  "Wrapped One"
                  "Convenience Food"
                  "8 oz. Wedge"
                  (November)

318. 1968   *KELLOGGS*
                  Cameraman: Larry Pizer
                  "Good morning, Sunday"
                  "Campers"
                  "Seaside"
                  "Brian"
                  "Boys"
                  "Winter"
                  (May/June)

319. 1968   *KELLOGGS*
                  "First day at school"
                  "Ironing"
                  "Telephone"
                  "Paper Round"
                  "Bananas"
                  (July/August)

320. 1969   *CAMPARI*
                  Cameraman: Larry Pizer.
                  "Daphne"
                  "Henry Henry"
                  "Sue You"
                  "Sidney"
                  "Reverse"
                  (July)

321. 1969 *KELLOGGS*

Cameraman: R. Paynter.
"Good morning, neighbour."
"Learner"
"Young Lady"
"Shoppers"
"Mechanic"
"Monday"
(August/September)

322. 1969 *GUINNESS*

Cameraman: Larry Pizer.
"Martians"
"Charabanc"
(December)

323. 1970 *FINDUS*

Cameraman: Larry Pizer. With Lucinda Curtis, Dorothea Philips, Christopher Coll, Trevor Martin, Fanny Carby, Hilda Fenemore.
"Kettle"
"Barbecue"
"Wine Goblets"
(August)

324. 1971 *PRESTIGE EWBANK*

Cameraman: Larry Pizer. With Jeremy Bullock, Therese McMurray, Connie Merrigold.
"Young Man"
(June)

325. 1971 *ALCAN*

Cameraman: Larry Pizer
"Chef MK II"
(October)

TELEVISION DRAMAS

326. 1971 *Home* by David Storey (WNET New York)

Decor by William McCrow. Music by Alan Price. Executive Producer: Jac Venza. With John Gielgud, Ralph Richardson, Dandy Nichols, Mona Washbourne, Warren Clarke

327. 1978 *The Old Crowd* by Alan Bennett (London Weekend Television)

Designed by Jim Weatherup. Producer: Stephen Frears. Production Manager: Mike McLoughlin.

With Rachel Roberts, Jill Bennett, Isabel Dean, Peter Jeffrey, John Moffatt, Cathleen Nesbitt, Valentine Dyall, Elspeth March, Philip Stone, Frank Grimes, Adele Leigh, David King, Peter Bennett, Jenny Quayle, Martyn Jacobs, James Ottaway.

THEATRE PRODUCTIONS

328. 1957   *The Waiting of Lester Abbs* by Kathleen Sully (Royal Court Theatre, London)

Production without decor (Sunday night performance). With Ian Bannen, Gladys Spencer, Catherine Willmer, Alun Owen, Alfred Burke, Anna Steele, Michael Hastings, Fanny Carby, Robert Stephens, and John Dexter.

329. 1959   *The Long and the Short and the Tall* by Willis Hall (Royal Court & New Theatre, London)

Decor, Alan Tagg. With Peter O'Toole, Robert Shaw, Ronald Fraser, Edward Judd, Bryan Pringle, Kenji Takaki, Alfred Lynch, and David Andrews.

330. 1959   *Jazzetry*, Poetry-and-Jazz by Christopher Logue and the Tony Kinsey Quintet. (Royal Court Theatre)

331. 1959   *The Trial of Cobb and Leach*, A musical play by Christopher Logue, music by Tony Kinsey and Bill Le Sage (Royal Court Theatre)

Production without decor (Sunday night performance). With George Rose, Shani Wallace, Shirley Cameron, Ronald Fraser, Bryan Pringle, Ann Beech, Peter O'Toole, and George Devine.

332. 1959   *Progress to the Park* by Alun Owen. (Royal Court Theatre)

Production without decor (Sunday night performance). Scenic desposition by Sean Kenny. With Harry H. Corbett, Margaret Tyzack, Tom Bell, Donald Donnelly, Keith Smith, Fanny Carby, Bee Duffell, Gerard Dynevor, and Donald Howarth. Music by The Temperance Seven.

333. 1959   *Dispersal* by A. L. Patterson (Belgrade Theatre, Coventry)

Decor by Sean Kenny. With Jill Bennett, Daniel Massey, John Lee, Cherry Morris, Ewan Hooper, and Stratford Johns.

334. 1959   *Serjeant Musgrave's Dance* by John Arden (Royal Court Theatre)

Decor by Jocelyn Herbert. Music by Dudley Moore. With Ian Bannen, Freda Jackson, Alan Dobie, Frank

Finlay, Donal Donnelly, Patsy Byrne, Harry Gwynn Davies, Colin Blakely, Jack Smethhurst, and Stratford Johns.

| 335. | 1960 | *The Lily White Boys* by Harry Cookson. (Royal Court Theatre) |

Lyrics by Christopher Logue. Music by Tony Kinsey and Bill Leage. Decor by Sean Kenny. Assistant Director: Anthony Page.

With Albert Finney, Georgia Brown, Monty Landis, Shirley Ann Field, Philip Locke, Ann Lynn, Willoughby Goddard, Ronnie Stevens, Barbara Hicks, Geoffrey Hibbert, and James Grout.

| 336. | 1960 | *Billy Liar* by Keith Waterhouse and Willis Hall. (Cambridge Theatre, London) |

Decor by Alan Tagg. With Albert Finney, Mona Washbourne, George A. Cooper, Jennifer Jayne, Juliet Cooke, Ethel Griffies, and Trevor Bannister. (Albert Finney succeeded by Tom Courtenay after nine months.)

| 337. | 1960 | *Trials by Logue* (Royal Court Theatre) |

Decor by Jocelyn Herbert

"Antigone" by Christopher Logue.

"The Trial of Cobb and Leech" by Logue, Kinsey and Le Sage (revived).

With Mary Ure, George Rose, Zoe Caldwell, Tony Selby, Peter Duguid, Derek Newark, Peter Holmes, and Dickie Owen.

| 338. | 1961 | *The Fire Raisers* (Biedermann and The Fire Raisers) by Max Frisch. (Royal Court Theatre) |

Decor by Alan Tagg. Music by Dudley Moore. With Alfred Marks, James Booth, Colin Blakely, Doris Hare, Ann Beech, Catherine Willmer, John Thaw, Henry Woolf, and Dickie Owen.

| 339. | 1961 | *Box and Cox* (Curtain Raiser) |

With James Booth, Colin Blakely, and Doris Hare.

| 340. | 1963 | *The Diary of a Madman* by Gogol. Adaptation by Lindsay Anderson and Richard Harris. (Royal Court Theatre) |

Decor by Voytak. Music by Carl Davis. With Richard Harris.

| 341. | 1964 | *Andorra* by Max Frisch. (The National Theatre at the Old Vic, London) |

Decor by John Bury. With Tom Courtenay, Cyril Cusack, Diana Wynyard, Robert Stephens, Lynn

		Redgrave, Colin Blakely, Derek Jacobi, Robert Lang, and Anthony Nicholls.

342.   1964   *Julius Caesar* by William Shakespeare. (Royal Court Theatre)

Decor by Jocelyn Herbert. Music by Marc Wilkinson. Assistant Director: Peter Gill. With Ian Bannen, T. P. McKenna, Daniel Massey, Paul Curren, Nan Munro, Sheila Allen, Graham Crowden, Anthony Hopkins, Ronald Pickup, Stephen Moore, John Dunn Hill, Petronella Barker, and Malcolm Reynolds.

343.   1966   *The Cherry Orchard,* by Anton Chekhov, translated by Elisaveta Fen. (Festival Theatre, Chichester)

Decor by Alan Tagg. Music by Mischa Donat. With Celia Johnson, Tom Courtenay, Hugh Williams, Zena Walker, Ray McAnally, Sarah Badel, Bill Fraser, John Standing, Catherine Willmer, Michael Burrell, John Laurie, Ben Kingsley, Peter Egan, Sheena Campbell, and Gordon Reid.

344.   1966   *Nie Do Obrony (Inadmissable Evidence)* by John Osborne, translated by Kazimierz Piotrowski. (Teatr Wzpolczesny—Contemporary Theatre, Warsaw)

Decor by Jocelyn Herbert. With Tadeusz Lomnicki, Mieczyslaw Pawlikowski, Mieczyslaw Gajda, Zofia Saretok, Barbara Wrzesinska, Renata Kossobudzka, and Zofia Mrozowska.

345.   1969   *In Celebration* by David Storey. (Royal Court Theatre)

Decor by Peter Docherty. With Alan Bates, James Bolam, Brian Cox, Bill Owen, Constance Chapman, Gabrielle Daye, and Fulton Mackay.

346.   1969   *The Contractor* by David Storey. (Royal Court and Fortune Theatre, London).

Decor by John Gunter. Lighting by Andy Phillips. With Bill Owen, T. P. McKenna, Philip Stone, Jim Norton, Constance Chapman, John Antrobus, Norma Jones, Billy Russell, Adele Strong, and Martin Shaw (at Fortune Theatre, Paul Moriarty).

347.   1970   *Home* by David Storey. (Royal Court and Apollo Theatre, London; Morosco Theatre, New York).

Decor by Jocelyn Herbert. Music by Alan Price. Lighting by Andy Phillips. With John Gielgud, Ralph Richardson, Dandy Nicholls, Mona Washbourne, and Warren Clarke (Warren Clarke succeeded by Graham Weston at the Morosco Theatre).

348. 1971   *The Changing Room* by David Storey. (Royal Court and Globe Theatre, London).

Decor by Jocelyn Herbert. Lighting by Andy Phillips. With Jim Norton, John Barrett, Edward Judd, David Dacre, Mark McManus, Barry Keegan, Brian Glover, Paul Dawkins, John Rae, Dave Hill, Frank Mills, Michael Elphick, Edward Peel, Geoffrey Hinsliff, Brian Lawson, Don McKillop, John Price, Alun Armstrong, Peter Childs, and Matthew Guinness.

349. 1973   *The Farm* by David Storey. (Royal Court and Mayfair Theatre, London).

Decor by Hayden Griffin. Music by Alan Price. Lighting by Nick Chelton. With Bernard Lee, Frank Grimes, Doreen Mantle, Patricia Healey, Prunella Gee, Lewis Collins, and Meg Davies.

350. 1974   *Life Class* by David Storey.(Royal Court and Duke of Yorks Theatre, London).

Decor by Jocelyn Herbert. Lighting by Nick Chelton. Music by Johann Sebastian Bach. With Alan Bates, Rosemary Martin, Brian Glover, Frank Grimes, Bob Peck, Gerald James, Gabrielle Lloyd, Paul Kelly, Stephen Bent, Sally Watts, David Lincoln, Brenda Cavendish, Stuart Rayner, and Maureen Callaghan.

351. 1975   *What the Butler Saw* by Joe Orton. (Royal Court and Whitehall Theatre, London).

Decor by Jocelyn Herbert. Music by Alan Price. Lighting by Nick Chelton. Assistant Director: Jon Plowman. With Michael Medwin, Betty Marsden, Valentine Dyall, Brian Glover, Jane Carr, and Kevin Lloyd.

352. 1975   *The Sea Gull* by Anton Chekhov, adaptation by Lindsay Anderson and Galina von Mack. (Lyric Theatre, London).

Decor by Alan Tagg. Lighting by Joe Davis. Assistant Director: Jon Plowman. With Joan Plowright, John Moffatt, Helen Mirren, Frank Grimes, Peter McEnery, Patricia Healey, Patsy Rowlands, Leonard Fenton, Neil Kennedy, and Kevin Stoney.

353. 1975   *The Bed Before Yesterday* by Ben Travers. (Lyric Theater, London)

Decor by Alan Tagg. Lighting by Joe Davis. Assistant Director: Jon Plowman. With Joan Plowright, John Moffitt, Helen Mirren, Frank Grimes, Leonard

Fenton, Royce Mills, Patsy Rowlands, and Gabrielle Daye.

354.   1977   *The Kingfisher*, by William Douglas Home. (Lyric Theatre, London).

Decor by Alan Tagg. Lighting by Joe Davis. Music by Alan Price. With Ralph Richardson, Celia Johnson, and Alan Webb. (Alan Webb succeeded by Frederick Farley).

ADDITIONAL FILM MATERIAL

355.   1969   *About The White Bus* directed by John Fletcher.

Edited and produced by Marlene Fletcher. Written by Howard Thompson. With the assistance and cooperation of Ian Wood, Heather Sutton, Walter Lasally, Gavrik Losey, Shelagh Delaney, Oscar Lewinstein, the unit and cast of *The White Bus*, Tony Richardson, Woodfall Films and United Artists, Stanley Reed, and the British Film Institute.

This film about the making of Anderson's *The White Bus* was shot by John Fletcher, who had worked with Anderson on *Thursday's Children* and *Every Day Except Christmas*. It was shot with a French Eclair 16 millimeter camera linked to a Nagra tape recorder and used an extra sensitive film stock. It took three years for Fletcher and his wife to edit. It finally emerged as one director's notebook on the work of another filmmaker.

356.   1973   "O Lucky Man!" Music and songs by Alan Price. Warner Brothers Records (BS2710). Composer and singer: Alan Price, with Colin Green, guitar; Dave Markee, bass guitar; and Clive Thacker, drums. Arranged and produced by Alan Price; Engineer: Keith Grant. Original sound track album with the lyrics for all of the songs used in the film *O Lucky Man!*, including "My Home Town" which was cut from the film.

ARTICLES BY ANDERSON

1947

357. "Angles of Approach." *Sequence*, 2 (Winter), 71-72.

Anderson states the outline of his critical credo. "It is the critic's first duty (and in a sense we are all critics) to perceive the object of a film and to judge its success in achieving that object." We are to do so without allowing "outside considerations—irrelevancies" from swaying our judgment. The first task of the artist is to create, to make us "jettison our own prejudices and viewpoints, and to accept those of the artist." There is only one angle of approach, one which covers that which is good and will not include the second-rate.

358. "The Manvell Aproach." *Sequence,* 2 (Winter), 34-35.
In this review of *20 Years of British Film* by Michael Balcon, Ernest Lundgren, Forsyth Hardy, and Roger Manvell, and the *Penguin Film Review II* and *III* edited by Roger Manvell, Anderson faults British film critics for their narrowness and lack of intelligence. Anderson attacks the smugness and the insularity of the *British Film* volume which is given over to "British Orthodox Film Boost-Group." Manvell himself has succumbed to this as well. He has lost his personal flair and enthusiasm trying to communicate with the simple-minded mass audience.

359. Review of *Paisa* (Ordinary People). *Sequence,* 2 (Winter), 30–31.
While acknowledging the vital sense of reality in Rossellini's film, Anderson is careful to distinguish this film from a documentary. The one major flaw in the film, in spite of its sincerity and truthfulness, is the lack of statement. Anderson wishes that Rossellini had stepped forward and made some sort of pronouncement to draw the film together, to give it unity. Anderson sees the "documentary approach" as inhibiting the artist from imposing his ideas on the raw material, from "exercising his right to shape and to exclude," and, in short, denying him the right to make a masterpiece.

1948

360. "Creative Elements." *Sequence,* 5 (Autumn), 8-12.
In this essay Anderson discusses the various creative elements which combine to make up a film. He also points out that one of the elementary duties of the critic is to isolate and evaluate the contribution of each element. Such analyses should aid the viewer in appreciating the merits of the film as well as clarifying the second-rate. The end result is to help the viewer more keenly enjoy the film because he understands it more exactly.

361. "The Need for Competence." *Sequence,* 3 (Spring), 34-35.
An unfavorable review of a pamphlet on film music from the British Film Institute. Anderson thinks that the pamphlet is too pedantically academic and loaded with jargon. He sees little reason to justify the need to study film music which Hans Keller does in his "The Need for Competent Film Music Criticism." The piece is too bombastic and, in the field of criticism, says Anderson, "it is important that competence should not be identified with display."

362. "A Possible Solution." *Sequence,* 3 (Spring), 7-10.
Pinpoints the ills of the British studio system as stemming from the corporate set-up of the motion picture companies. Artists, including film artists, do not work well within such an organization. Anderson believes that British film needs to be rejuvenated by an avant-garde movement of independent productions. Unfortunately, the matter of distribution still remains, but perhaps through the film societies and specialist cinemas, some measure of economic support could be built up. The problem is complex, but he feels the need to rejuvenate British film and to recapture something "fresh, spontaneous, individual."

363. Review of *Sciuscia*. *Sequence*, 4 (Summer), 38-39.
  Praises de Sica's "tremendous actuality," "honesty," and "passionate pleading for what we have come to term the human values." Chiefly, however, it is his "impulse of generous and uncompromising emotion" which gives his films their force, a force unknown to Hollywood or the British film industry.

364. Review of *Strange Voyage*. *Sequence*, 5 (Autumn), 42-43.
  Praises this small-scale independent production for its charm and freshness. The film was made by a group of American ex-service men who combined talents and money for the project. The film, although a "little" one, impressed Anderson as a remarkably promising one, and while watching it he frequently felt "that odd shiver of pleasure which is the effect of poetry anywhere—on the printed page or on the screen."

365. "What Goes On." *Sequence*, 4 (Summer), 44-45.
  This review of John Collier's *A Film in the Making* will call to mind Anderson's similar project, *Making of a Film: The Story of "Secret People" (see* no. 381), of four years later. Anderson praises Collier for providing the reading public with an idea of the "intimidating" complexity of filmmaking within a British studio "which aims at good as well as profitable pictures."

1949

366. "British Cinema: The Descending Spiral." *Sequence*, 7 (Spring), 6-11.
  "Perhaps the tendency is to treat the films of one's own country like its prophets—with less than justice. We are so close to them as, week by week, they churn out of the studios for our inspection; and now that their excellence has become almost an economic and political necessity (so that film criticism is regarded by many as a form of national service) the temptation to slash, to sneer rebelliously, is almost irresistible." Anderson begins his analysis of the British film scene by announcing that he for one does not intend to generalize from "every boring quickie" turned out by the British studios. This balanced analysis of the contemporary film situation in Great Britain contains Anderson's conclusion that the impact of the documentary school has been slight, and that in spite of some minor changes in format, British films still seem limited. He calls for a healthier art to come out of this healthier industry.

367. "The Film Front." *Sequence*, 8 (Summer), 91.
  Brief review of Basil Wright's book *The Use of the Film*, in which Anderson praises Wright's "admirable consciousness, justice, and common sense" in dealing with his subject matter. He laments the lack of depth or exploration of some of Wright's main points, but says the book should "provide a balanced and stimulating basis for discussion."

368. "Film Review: *Louisiana Story*." *Sequence*, 6 (Winter), 38-40.
  Praises Flaherty's enchanted world in *Louisiana Story*, and the harmony with which theme and incident are preserved "in perfect balance." He also feels that the use of non-professional actors in the film is one of the most "completely successful examples" in film history. "At a time when so much magic has gone out of the world, when the faculty of wonder seems likely to disappear altogether, it is

not surprising that the innocent eye of childhood should commend itself more strongly than ever as a subject for the artist."

369. "Films of Alfred Hitchcock." *Sequence,* 9 (Autumn), 113-124.
A Brief overview of Hitchcock's career, emphasizing in particular the change in style caused by Hitchcock's move to Hollywood in the 1930s. In spite of Hollywood's offering him far greater opportunities and Hitchcock's use of the superior technical resources of Hollywood, Anderson feels that his films since the move have lacked the wholeness of the earlier British ones. The balance between content and style which characterizes those films is missing in his American productions. The enlargement of his style made possible by the American studios and their financial strength has not been accompanied by an equal growth in sensibility and subject matter.

370. Review of *The History of Mr. Polly. Sequence,* 7 (Spring), 41-42.
The film misses Well's subtlety and turns the novel into farce. In spite of the quality of the script, the music, and the photography, the movie misses "the pattern of the whole"; the film's total gesture seems to be lacking.

371. "The Studio That Begs to Differ," in *Film and Theatre Today: The European Scene.* London: The Saturn Press, pp. 16-19.
This piece contains a brief history and analysis of the Ealing Studios. Anderson catalogues the strengths of the studio's films: "a relatively high standard of intelligence and taste in their writing," a "concern for realism and probability," and a "general modesty of their approach." The virtues, however, may become a handicap. Anderson sees the possibility that only producing "good films" might preclude the studio from producing any really "great" ones.

1950

372. "The Director's Cinema?" *Sequence,* 12 (Autumn), 6-11, 37.
Discusses the true role of the director in the cinema, in response to a letter criticizing his review of John Ford's *She Wore a Yellow Ribbon.* Anderson not only defends his affection for the film and for Ford as a director, but he also enters into the controversy about the relative importance of the film director in the construction of the movie. Anderson comments on some remarks between Thorold Dickinson, a British director, and Howard Kock, a Hollywood scriptwriter, on the merits of the screenwriter in the film. Anderson acknowledges the importance of the writer, but admits that the overall creative hand belongs to the director.

373. Letter to the Editor. *Sight and Sound,* 19 (July), 264.
Anderson points out an inaccuracy in a review of *All the King's Men* which had appeared in *Sight and Sound.* He also Praises Abraham Polonsky's script work on *Body and Soul,* which was largely responsible for the film's success.

374. "Notes at Cannes." *Sequence,* 10 (New Year), 184-186.
Contains a rather impressionistic survey of the Cannes Film Festival with brief commentary by Anderson on the various films he saw. For example, he is not convinced that *The Third Man* is really worth the acclamation it is receiving. Morally, at least, he is opposed to its "fashionable defeatism": "Reed zithering while Europe disintegrates?"

375. "Retrospective Review: *Wagonmaster* and *Two Flags West.*" *Sight and Sound,* 19 (December), 333-334.

Anderson Praises Ford's *Wagonmaster,* stating "he has composed, with the simplicity of greatness, another of his poems to the pioneering spirit." *Two Flags West,* directed by Robert Wise, is plagued by "indecisive scripting" and a lack of dynamism. Wise has achieved no more than a "series of effects." "A comparison of the images of *Wagonmaster* and *Two Flags West* points out the difference between the expressive poet's eye, and the elegant, superficial skill of the *decorateur.*"

376. "*They Were Expendable* and John Ford." *Sequence,* 11 (Summer), 18-31.

This long essay on John Ford, occasioned by the review of his film *They Were Expendable,* contains Anderson's reasons as to why Ford should be considered one of the world's major filmmakers. "Ford has always found his true image of reality in this world, not in the deliberately fashioned symbolism of a literary invention; his symbols arise naturally out of the ordinary, the everyday; it is by familiar places, traditions and themes that his imagination is most happily stimulated." His natural poetic ability plus his control over the medium allows Ford to create films "which can be enjoyed by anyone, regardless of cultural level, who has retained his sensitivity and subscribes to values primarily humane."

1951

377. "Goldwyn at Claridges." *Sequence,* 13 (New Year), 9-10.

Anderson gives his impressions of Samuel Goldwyn based on an interview with the American film executive at Claridges in London. He found Goldwin frank and assured. He was less interested in analyzing his films than in merely talking about them. He offered Anderson advice about how to increase the circulation of *Sequence* ("Get some pretty girls inside"). Anderson sees Goldwyn's great talent as being in tune with the public who go to movies; he is blessed "with that divine confidence in the rightness (moral, aesthetic, commercial) of his own intuition."

378. "John Ford." *Films in Review,* 2 (February), 5-16.

An abridged version of Anderson's article for *Sequence,* "*They Were Expendable* and John Ford." This version omits the review of *They Were Expendable* and includes the section on Ford's career (*see* no. 376).

1952

379. "As the Critics Like It; Some Personal Choices." *Sight and Sound,* 22, no. 2 (October-December), 58.

A number of film critics were asked for their list of the ten films which had impressed them most. Here is Anderson's list: 1. *Earth;* 2. *They Were Expendable* (Ford); 3. *Zéro de Conduite, Atlante* (Vigo); 4. *Childhood of Maxim Gorki;* 5. *Grapes of Wrath, Bicycle Thieves;* 6. *Louisiana Story, The River* (Renoir); 7. *Fires Were Started* (Jennings); 8. *La Règle de Jeu, Le Jour se Leve;* 9. *Douce* (Aurant-Lara), *Antoine et Antoinette* (Becker), *Force of Evil* (Polonsky); and 10. *Meet Me in St. Louis* (Minnelli).

380. "Casque D'or." *Sight and Sound,* 22, no. 2 (October-December), 75-77.

Highly complimentary review of Jacques Becker's film. Anderson describes the love story containing Becker's exploration of emotional geography in which he traces "the varying currents and strange depths which characterize the most intimate human relations." The style is superb; the command of tempo is masterly; and the "images are of continuous but simple richness."

381. *Making a Film: The Story of "Secret People."* Chronicled and edited by Lindsay Anderson. London: Allen and Unwin, 223 pp.

This is a day-by-day account of the filming of Thorold Dickinson's film, *Secret People.* Anderson provides an introduction and running commentary. Also appended is a copy of the shooting script by Dickinson and Wolfgang Wilhelm. Anderson supplies everything imaginable: shooting schedules, dope sheets, cross plot information, and background on just about every aspect of the film.

382. "Minnelli, Kelly and *An American in Paris.*" *Sequence,* 14 (New Year), 36-38.

Anderson uses this review of *An American in Paris* to discuss the Hollywood musical and Minnelli's break with what Anderson calls its rigid conventions and machine-like efficiency. Minnelli has added genuine feeling to the form, and, with Gene Kelly, has "civilized" the American musical. *An American in Paris* is not up to their usual form but Anderson hopes that they will return to it with their next film.

383. "The Quiet Man." *Sequence,* 14 (New Year), 32-37.

An account of Anderson's interview with John Ford who was legendary for *not* granting interviews. Anderson's conclusion is that Ford is indeed impossible to interview. There is a nice exchange between the critic and the moviemaker about the merits of *They Were Expendable.* Anderson liked it (*see* no. 376) and Ford pretends to think it stinks and admits that he has not seen the final version. Ford had been to Ireland making *The Quiet Man* where Anderson interviewed him. Anderson concludes the article by quoting Ford's assertion that he really wanted to be a tugboat captain. Anderson writes: "But God made him a poet, and he must make the best of that."

384. "The Quiet Man." *Sight and Sound,* 22, no. 1 (July-September), 24-26.

Anderson is quite taken by John Ford's *The Quiet Man.* He praises Ford's vivid sense of locality, the adventurous use of color, and his impeccable sense of pace and proximity. Ford's style is marvelously lucid and the form tight. The film abounds in scenes of poetic originality and excitement.

385. Review of *Murder in the Cathedral. Sight and Sound,* 22, no. 1 (July-September), 43-44.

Anderson is unimpressed by this rather sententious book containing the script of T.S. Eliot's play/screenplay, *Murder in the Cathedral.* It is obvious from his introduction to the volume that Eliot knows nothing about the film, Anderson observes. In addition, the screenplay is nothing more than a sketchy annotated version of the play. Anderson is further put off by the collection of trivia which the authors have collected for this volume (relics, Anderson calls them). It is an unsatisfactory volume for the serious student of film.

1953

386. "Cannes 1953." *Sight and Sound,* 23, no. 1 (July-September), 18-20.

A report on the Cannes Film Festival, both the films and what Anderson calls the second level of the festivities: "personalities, gossip, conspiracies." He singles out a number of films for special notice, some his favorites and some the prize winners, but they are not necessarily the same ones. The real achievement of the festival, though, is to bring together the enthusiasts, like Anderson himself, and with them it is possible to get beneath the superficialities.

387. "Encounter with Prévert." *Sight and Sound,* 23, no. 1 (July-September), 4.
Short letter from France where Anderson has had a meeting with Jacques Prévert. Anderson gives his impressions of the French filmmaker and describes how Prévert likes English poets and the *un*reality of British films.

388. "Only Connect: Some Aspects of the Work of Humphrey Jennings." *Sight and Sound,* 23, no. 4 (April-June), 181-183, 186.
In this warm appreciation of the work of Humphrey Jennings, Anderson stresses the importance of the war in providing a focus for Jennings' film style. Anderson suggests that it took an event of the magnitude of the Second World War to kindle his passions. Jennings' style, so intimately tied to the everyday people of Great Britain during the war, makes him a poet in film, perhaps the "only real poet the British cinema has yet produced."
Reprinted: "Some Aspects of the Work of Humphrey Jennings" (*see* no. 440).

389. Review of *Birth of a Nation. Sight and Sound,* 22, no. 3 (January-March), 129-30.
Anderson wonders, on this occasion of the release of a new theater version of the classic film, whether or not it has retained its entertainment value. He deplores the fact that the addition of the sound track has necessitated the running of the film at sound speed, thus distorting the acting styles of the principals, and he finds the latter half, as in *Gone With the Wind,* a disappointment. The racism seems terribly dated now, and in spite of the film's ending, which has a "stylistic *tour de force,*" the melodrama and hysteria are distasteful.

390. Review of *Come Back, Little Sheba. Sight and Sound,* 22, no. 4 (April-June), 196-197.
Criticizes this film for its slavish adherence to the stage production. At the same time, he praises Shirley Booth's performance in the leading role. Anderson feels that Daniel Mann was too inexperienced to make independent decisions on the film. As a result, it is a "theatrical handling of an efficient, orthodox, quite impersonal decoupage."

391. Review of *The Sun Shines Bright. Sight and Sound,* 23, no. 2 (October-December), 88-89.
This is one of John Ford's films which he made for himself alone, not the public or the critics or the studios, just himself. The film embodies Ford's personal statement, his personal feelings—"those qualities which seem each year to grow rarer in the American cinema." Although the photography is not his best, the images have the "forcefulness, lucidity and power of suggestion" that one has come to expect from Ford. "It is impossible not to wonder at the way Ford has managed to preserve so freshly, all these years, this power to move and delight, this *poesie du coeur*. The phrase is Cocteau's; it evokes precisely the kind of positive poetry, full of faith and love of life, which Ford continues to create, alone."

392. Review of *What Price Glory? Sight and Sound*, 23, no. 3 (January-March), 131.

In spite of Ford's touch, this remake is not as good as the original silent classic. Although reminiscent in its "mingling of humour and sentiment, knockabout and sentimentality" of *Tobacco Road*, the film never quite coalesces into a poetic whole. It is nevertheless sometimes funny and occasionally stirring, and "there is none of that pervasive deadness which afflicts so many Hollywood films nowadays."

1954

393. "Book Reviews: *A Tree Is a Tree* by King Vidor." *Sight and Sound*, 23, no. 4 (April-June), 217-218.

Anderson notes that most Hollywood directors do not talk about their trade, and, in spite of the fact that King Vidor announces that he *will* talk in his autobiography, there is little in it that is very revealing. He spends most of his time writing about his need to do pictures, about hope, and the common man. Anderson also finds it a bit sad to look back on a Hollywood more assured and less sophisticated, the Hollywood of Vidor's best films: *The Big Parade, The Crowd*, and *Hallelujah*. The book reveals enough about the director to warrant a rediscovery, at least of the early films.

394. "Correspondence: Straight Questions." *Sight and Sound*, 24, no. 4 (October-December), 107-108.

In this letter to the editor, Anderson complains about a series of articles John Grierson was publishing in *Sight and Sound*. He objects to the series for a number of reasons, but largely because Grierson seems to be so sloppy in his use of facts and in his critical analysis. Anderson, for one, was singled out by Grierson as an example of the new critical school which he deplores. Anderson asks Grierson to stop name-calling and to get down to cases.

395. "French Critical Writing." *Sight and Sound*, 24, no. 2 (October-December), 105.

Anderson praises the French for the seriousness with which they discuss art, including the cinema. This is especially evident in the series of film books issued by Editions du Cerf under the title of "7c Art." "Admirably produced, and very well illustrated, these little books show a standard of specialized knowledge and gusto quite beyond anything one can imagine being done in this country." Anderson also praises two French film journals, *Cahiers du Cinéma* and *Positif*.

396. "Perspectives at Cannes." *Sight and Sound*, 24, no. 1 (July-September), 6-8.

"Indeed, judged simply on the films shown, it was not an outstanding occasion. The technical standard of work was high: films were well shot, well cut, the syntax of cinema correctly employed. But what struck one was the rarity with which this form of language was freshly, surprisingly, stimulatingly used." If anything did stand out, it was the group of films from behind the Iron Curtain. They were politically concerned but were "alive nevertheless with true human feeling and idealism." Anderson found that refreshing after the overwhelming commercialism of the western films.

397. Review of *The Adventures of Robinson Crusoe. Sight and Sound*, 24, no. 2 (October-December), 86-87.

Anderson is pleased with Buñuel's tight direction of this film. His re-emergence as a director, unlike some others recently, has been a happy event. For Anderson, Buñuel is an "artist of fresh, still developing talent," and *The Adventures of Robinson Crusoe* is "a poetic film, with a purity of style that marks it as the statement of a man of integrity, direct, uncompromised."

398. Review of *The Big Heat*. *Sight and Sound*, 24, no. 1 (July-September), 36.
Anderson finds this Fritz Lang thriller containing the virtues his films had been lacking: "tautness and speed; modesty of intention; intelligent, craftsman-like writing." The film proves that, when his interest is engaged, Lang "still has at his control the technique of a master."

399. Review of *Dieu Au Cinema*. *Sight and Sound*, 23, no. 3 (January-March), 163.
This is the review of Amedee Ayfre's book which Anderson was preparing when he met with Prévert and which prompted Prévert's comments on religion and film (*see* no. 387). Anderson begins this piece by announcing that he had expected this volume to be a defense of Catholic propaganda in films. Instead, he found a rather well-done study of "the expression of religious views in films from a strictly aesthetic point of view," and an evaluation of the relationship between the success of that presentation and the quality of the aesthetic values.

400. Review of *Falbalas* and *Rendezvous de Juillet*. *Sight and Sound*, 24, no. 2 (October-December), 90-91.
Anderson laments the butchering which Jacques Becker's *Rendezvous de Juillet* received at the hands of the British distributors. In an earlier account of this film Anderson had praised Becker's style and presentation. Becker is a director of *ambiance*, one who is fascinated "with the specialized forms of human behavior, with the peculiar conventions and apparatus through which individual sections of society express their ways of living." In spite of his apparently humane approach, there is something in Becker which remains "uncommitted."

401. Review of *Madame De . . . . Sight and Sound*, 23, no. 4 (April-June), 196-197.
Unlike a number of European directors who have gotten lost making films in Hollywood, Max Ophuls has gone astray by returning to Europe after making some rather remarkable films in America. Anderson feels that the fluid style and mobile camera which characterize Ophuls' work have gotten out of hand since his return to Europe. The heady success of *La Ronde* and the sophisticated European atmosphere have contributed to Ophuls' current stylistic mannerisms.

1955

402. "Cannes 1955." *Sight and Sound*, 25, no. 1 (Summer), 48-50.
"What was Cannes 1955 *really* like?" begins Anderson's report of the International Film Festival. There was much of the same argument about the use of cinemascope, unworkable for intimate films, useful for documentaries; a refreshing exposure to some little-seen Japanese films, especially those of Kenzo Mizoguchi; the usual smattering of disappointing films from France, Germany, and Great Britain; and the usual number of previously unknown films which are fresh and unassuming and restore one's faith in the possibilities of cinema.

403. "The Last Sequence of *On the Waterfront*." *Sight and Sound*, 24, no. 3 (January-March), 127-130.

Anderson criticizes Elia Kazan for his insincere and socially irresponsible film. Unlike most reviewers, Anderson sees the triumph of Terry Malloy at the conclusion of the film as an indictment of the mass, the people. Although *On the Waterfront* is a bad film, it is not without importance, largely because of its overwhelming acceptance. Unfortunately, instead of seeing the triumph of social justice at the end of the film as the director had intended, Anderson sees in it a vision of defeat for collective action. The style of the movie also reinforces its falsity. Anderson feels that the film relies on "emotional tricks" for too much of its impact. He compares this film to Abraham Polonsky's *Force of Evil*. Polonsky's film attracted little attention, but stated with greater force the same theme Kazan was aiming at in *On the Waterfront*. (For the barrage of dissenting opinions occasioned by this review, *see also* nos. 27, 29, 31, 32, 33, and 34).

404. Review of *Drive a Crooked Road* and *Pushover*. *Sight and Sound*, 24, no. 3 (January-March), 144.

Anderson is impressed with Richard Quine's first two films. He finds these movies reminiscent of the old days when Hollywood turned out products which fulfilled the audience's "expectation of seeing a story told in pictures, black and white and incisive, aiming simply to please." He much prefers *Drive a Crooked Road* to *Pushover* because of its bite and intelligence and its good storytelling. Both films, however, have a "wry disenchantment, rather sad quality about them which betrays the presence behind the camera of an individual, a human being, and a sensitive one."

405. Review of *Human Desire*. *Sight and Sound*, 24, no. 4 (Spring), 198.

In this short review of Fritz Lang's latest film, Anderson laments the movie's final disintegration while praising the acting (Glenn Ford and Gloria Grahame), and the harshness and lack of gloss which so effectively underlie the film's sense of futility and failure.

406. Review of *Mr. Roberts*. *Sight and Sound*, 25, no. 3 (Winter), 149.

Mr. Roberts, Anderson writes, is a "[p]atchy diversion, rather padded out, occasionally bright and finally quite amusing." He does lament the lack of Ford's sure hand except in the exteriors, and the underlying "divergence of sensibility under the surface of the comedy."

407. Review of *Positif* and *Cahiers du Cinéma*. *Sight and Sound*, 24, no. 3 (January-March), 161.

In this review of the latest issues of these two French film journals, Anderson reverses his earlier opinion about the quality of their writing about cinema (*see* no. 395). He finds them containing "certain vices endemic in French criticism" and therefore worthy of attention. The current issue of *Positif* reflects the French naiveté about the need to write films well before they are shot, and the relationship between most Hollywood directors and their projects. *Cahiers du Cinéma* now reflects the eccentric enthusiasms of the "covey of bright young things" who have taken it over. The magazine is less concerned with cinema than with their individual reactions to cinema.

408. Review of *A Time Out of War*. *Sight and Sound*, 24, no. 4 (Spring), 197-198.

Anderson praises this modest film by Denis Sanders, a recent UCLA graduate. Made with little money and only three actors, the film nevertheless has a poetic quality about it. The total impact of the film adds up to a "solemn little elegy, with purity of feeling, a distinct individuality of approach that is rare, touchingly dignified."

1956

409. "Film Reviews: *The Searchers*." *Sight and Sound*, 26, no. 2 (Autumn), 94-95.

Anderson begins this review with the following: "Great men who fail habitually achieve more than lesser men who succeed; and films by great directors that miss their mark are often more interesting—more meaningful—than spotless but commonplace successes." Although *The Searchers* begins with promise, there is an "absence of feeling, of inner conviction" which makes it hollow. Ford seems to lack a theme and, even though he is back in the familiar territory of Monument Valley, there is a lack of intensity. "When belief is lacking, not all the technique in the world can hide the fact."

410. "Notes From Sherwood." *Sight and Sound*, 26, no. 3 (Winter), 159-160.

This essay was written when Anderson completed shooting the episodes for The Robin Hood television series (*see* nos. 299-303). This was the first time Anderson had worked in a studio, and he found the experience exhilarating. Unlike his experience with documentaries, he was under a good deal more pressure to shoot fast lest he waste time and money. He also describes working with the trained technicians and the stock company of actors, while trying to bring it all together as the director.

411. "Panorama at Cannes."*Sight and Sound*, 26, no. 1 (Summer), 16-21.

In this report Anderson finds the festival at Cannes, despite its chicanery, snobbery, and "distasteful publicity-hunting," a wonderfully uplifting experience." [T]here was the marvellous, heartening opportunity of witnessing the undiminished vitality of this medium which we in this country [Britain] are in danger of crassly allowing to run to waste." He expresses excitement about films by De Sica, Satyajit Ray, and disappointment in the American and the French entries. Anderson is particularly taken by a young Hungarian director, Zoltan Fabri, who uses the cinema poetically.

412. "Periodicals." *Sight and Sound*, 25, no. 4 (Spring), 217.

In this review of *Cinema '56* and *Positif*, Anderson contrasts the lively and intelligent *Cinema '56*, with its informative writing and admirably exhaustive approach, to *Positif*, with its "high-pitched, exhibitionist tone" and muddled layout. "There are times, it must be admitted, when the relentless pressure of so much criticism, counter-criticism and counter-counter-criticism becomes unbearable, and one is tempted to write off the whole pursuit as a sterile occupation."

413. Review of *Panorama du Film Noir Americain* by Raymond Borde and Étiènne Chaumeton. *Sight and Sound*, 25, no. 4 (Spring), 162.

Anderson is impressed by this French study of the American *film noir*. The authors show that the movement had a "coherence of style and a depth of implication considerably more serious" than British critics have been willing to admit. The only cavil with the book that Anderson has is that the moral drawn from "this school of violence and perverted eroticism" has been inferential rather than explicit, and he wishes that the handling of the films had been done in something more than catalogue fashion.

414. "Stand Up! Stand Up!" *Sight and Sound,* 26, no. 2 (Autumn), 63-93.
In this essay Anderson tries to formulate his principles as a film critic. Unlike a number of his contemporaries, he does not feel the need to remove his personal feelings and enthusiasms from his criticism. Anderson believes very strongly that a critic must be committed, politically and personally. "Essentially, in fact, there is no such thing as uncommitted criticism, any more than there is such a thing as insignificant art." Cinema is of the world and in it, and the critic should not remain silent about his commitments to the society out of which the cinema springs.

415. "Venice." *Sight and Sound,* 26, no. 2 (Autumn), 86-87.
The policy of allowing a panel of judges to choose the films to be shown at the Venice film festival is fraught with problems, according to Anderson. This procedure only has served to heighten the problems of overcrowding and shortage of worthy films brought about by the proliferation of film festivals. The one this year is not as dominated by commercial films as the one last year but there are not many good films, either. Anderson remains impressed by the Japanese entries.

1957

416. "Correspondence: A Distinguished List." *Sight and Sound,* 27, no. 2 (Autumn), 105.
This letter to the editor contains a notice from the gala opening of The National Film Theatre which Anderson thinks should have a wider circulation.

417. "Discoveries at Cannes." *Sight and Sound,* 27, no. 1 (Summer), 24-25, 28.
Anderson expresses enthusiasm about the remarkable new talent he discovered at the Cannes festival in 1957. The three most important new finds are from East Germany, Poland, and Argentina. Anderson says that the emergence of these filmmakers shows "how many people working in this enormously difficult medium are managing to defeat pressures and restrictions, and to produce work which genuinely reflects the spirit and struggle of our world." The images he saw are troubled and honest but not defeatist. He is most impressed by Andrej Wajda's *Kanal,* and its warmth and belief, "the dedicated sincerity of the playing, and the whole poetic spirit of the picture."

418. "Ten Feet Tall." *Sight and Sound,* 27, no. 1 (Summer), 34-36.
Anderson uses this review of some new American films to assess the trends in Hollywood. The decline in vitality of the American films has been accompanied by an influx of new directorial talent from television. If the old Hollywood is plagued by a sense of defeat, these new talents, mostly from New York, are creating an optimism, an idealism without romance. Anderson reviews *A Man Is Ten Feet Tall* by Martin Ritt, *Fear Strikes Out* by Robert Mulligan, *Twelve Angry Men* by Sidney Lumet, and *Bachelor Party* by Delbert Mann. In spite of the fact that the films contain a certain constriction, an overuse of the closeup, for instance, imported from television, they are fresh and exciting.

419. "Two Inches Off the Ground." *Sight and Sound,* 27, no. 3 (Winter), 131-133.

This review of the Japanese film was occasioned in part by a season of such films at the National Theatre. Anderson notes the way Japanese directors have modified the traditional Western notions of movement and pacing in film to accord with the Oriental perspective. Such exposure to alien notions of the film art have obliged European directors to reconsider and redefine technique. The refinement of the Japanese films creates an intimate relationship between the viewer and the cinema, closer to that enjoyed by novelist and reader than the *metteur-en-scène* has with his audience. In describing Mizoguchi's *Tokyo Story,* Anderson uses the following sentence: "For what we have here is a work that expresses in every image, and in the precise *growth* (as opposed to *force*) of its movement, a whole attitude to living, an attitude that comprehends, in the sense both of understanding and embracing, the painful necessities as well as the joys of existence."

420. "The Critical Issue: A Discussion Between Paul Rotha, Basil Wright, Lindsay Anderson, Penelope Houston." *Sight and Sound,* 27, no. 6 (Autumn), 271-275, 330.

Sight and Sound convened this conference to discuss film publications in Britain, beginning with *Close Up* which was first published in 1932. Anderson summarizes what the editors were trying to do with *Sequence* in the late forties and early fifties: they were trying to re-establish the aesthetic in film criticism and to reassert the primacy of the artistic function of film over its sociological or political function. Anderson now is alarmed at the passivity of the younger generation. All of the panelists agree that unless some new and innovative voices were raised in defense of film, the industry faced stagnation.

1958

421. "Get Out and Push!," in *Declaration.* Edited by Tom Maschler. New York: E. P. Dutton, pp. [136]-160.

In this rather political piece, Anderson calls for a reorganization of the traditional middle-class British film to include the other three-fourths of the population of the British Isles who have been excluded from serious treatment by the film industry. He calls on British filmmakers to tackle some of the problems which have been ignored by the industry in the name of a rather tepid humanism. In fact, Anderson notes the industry might be characterized as "snobbish, anti-intellectual, emotionally inhibited, willfully blind to the conditions and problems of the present, dedicated to an out-of-date, exhausted ideal." It is now time for British cinema to be regenerated, to fight for the values of humanism.

422. Review of *The Last Hurrah. Sight and Sound,* 28 (Spring), 93.

Anderson begins, "As one gets older, and the feeling increases that one has seen it all before, there seems to be only one thing left that can justify an abiding concern with the cinema: I mean its poetry." He finds Ford's latest film a disappointment. It does not have the poetry he has come to expect from Ford. "What do we mean by poetry? We mean intensity, emotional force, compression of style, that glow of imagination and feeling that transforms fact into symbol, story into myth." That is what Ford should be doing, transforming fact into symbol; he should be making "allegories, fairy stories, poems." Anderson hopes he will return to the West where he belongs.

423. "Three to Cheer For," in *International Film Annual No. 2.* Edited by William Whitebait. New York: Doubleday, pp. 79-86.

Anderson makes the case for independent or non-commercial films in his critique of Richard Williams' *The Little Ireland,* Claude Chabrol's *Le beau Serge,* and Andrzej Wajda's *Kanal.* Each was produced out of the western studio system; each was made for the sake of making a good film and not for profit. Williams pieced his film together on top of other jobs he took to make money. Chabrol used his considerable personal fortune to finance his film, and Wajda worked within the Polish film unit, a government operation which does not rely on commercial success for its financing. Such spirited and independent productions give the critic ammunition for supporting his call for change in the present system. "A better system is what we need, in which the good works which somehow continue to be created by the faith and persistence of the few, can achieve the showing they deserve."

1959

424. "The Filmmaker & the Audience: Replies to a Questionnaire," in *Film: Book 1: The Audience and the Filmmaker.* Edited by Robert Hughes New York: Grove Press, pp. 36-38.

Anderson supplies answers to several questions about audience appeal, encouraging and discouraging developments in film, and the like. Anderson's answer is premised on the assumptions that British film has always been and remains "conformist and class-bound," which limits those films to the middle-class mind, "orthodox, respectable, and 'nice.'" He finds British films stagnant for two reasons: "a reactionary social attitude," and "a total lack of showmanship and 'flair' on the part of almost everyone concerned with [them]" (*see* no. 427).

1961

425. "Pre-Renaissance." *International Theatre Annual,* no. 5, pp. [170]-186.

In this article about the English theater, Anderson makes references to the differences between theater and film. The audience is not passive in theater, for example. He also briefly mentions the influence of the presence of cinema on theater.

1963

426. "Sport, Life, and Art." *Films and Filming,* 9, no. 5 (February), 15-18.

In this essay occasioned by the making of *This Sporting Life,* Anderson writes about the emergence of film and the state of the cinema in Britain. He feels that the job of the artist is to disturb the audience, which is something his film will do. He also renounces any ambitions he had in the past to be a film critic; in fact, he says that "the remnants of my critical and polemical past which still survive in people's memories often prove rather embarrassing."

1967

427. "The Film Maker and the Audience," in *Film Makers on Film Making.* Edited by Harry Geduld. Bloomington, Ind.: Indiana University Press, pp. 276-278.

Reprint of an earlier article (*see* no. 424).

1969

428. "The Method of John Ford," in *The Emergence of Film Art.* Edited by Lewis Jacobs. New York: Hopkinson and Blake, pp. 230-245.
Reprint from *Sequence,* Summer 1950 (*see* no. 376).

429. "Notes for a Preface," in *If . . . : a Film* by Lindsay Anderson and David Sherwin. New York: Simon and Schuster, pp. 9-13.
In this preface Anderson explains the background of the film *If...*, acknowledging that some of it is autobiographical, but denying that the film is meant to be literal. Anderson mentions his influences: *Zéro de Conduite,* Brecht, John Ford, and Humphrey Jennings. The switching back and forth between color and black and white was an accident of finances. Anderson includes a brief account of the censorship problems the film faced in various countries. He also admits that the boys in the film, far from being rebels in a modern sense, are romantics; not anti-heroes, but old-fashioned boys.

1970

430. "Guildford School of Art: From Mr. Lindsay Anderson and Others." The *Times* (London) (20 September), p. 9.
A letter to the editor in which Anderson, among others, protests the treatment of some 40 teachers dismissed from the Guildford School of Art in 1968. The signers of this letter call for an inquiry into the affair and a quick settlement to a situation which they feel has gone on too long.

431. Quotation, in *The Lonely Artist: A Critical Introduction to the Films of Lester James Peries* by Philip Coorey. Ceylon: Lake House Investments Ltd., p. vi.
A brief quote by way of a preface from a remark made by Anderson during the Third International Film Festival in New Delhi where one of Peries' films won the Critics' Prize and the Golden Peacock in 1965. Anderson describes Peries as the lonely artist of Ceylon whose *Changes in the Village* "[a]stonished the Slavs with its elegiac, near Chekhovian grace."

432. Quotation, in *The Movies as Medium* by Lewis Jacobs. New York: Farrar, Strauss, & Giroux, p. 3.
Single quotation from Anderson's article, "Creative Elements" (*see* no. 360).

1971

433. "Financial Support for Film-Makers From Mr. Lindsay Anderson and Others." The *Times* (London) (15 August), p. 13.
Anderson and others demand that the government supply a large loan under the 1970 Films Act to the National Film Finance Corporation to finance British films. They feel that this is an opportunity to pull the British film industry out of its financial doldrums and provide the way for a strong and independent industry.

434. "John Ford." *Cinema,* 6, no. 3 (Spring), 23-26.
This is the monograph on John Ford which Anderson was commissioned to write in 1955 for a series of such volumes to be issued by *Sight and Sound.* Due to a

lack of funds, the project was abandoned, but Anderson's finished volume is printed here for the first time. Gavin Lamert has written a short introduction. The monograph is longer than the previous pieces published by Anderson on Ford, and contains a more detailed and far-reaching survey of Ford's career. The conclusions he draws about Ford, however, are substantially the same which he had been writing for years.

1972

435. "The Seventh Seal," in *Focus on The Seventh Seal*. Edited by Birgitta Steene. Englewood Cliffs, N.J.: Prentice-Hall, pp. 138-139.
Reprint of an earlier piece originally published in *Edinburgh Film Festival Catalogue*, 1957.

1973

436. "Crisis in Film Industry: From Mr. Lindsay Anderson and Others." The *Times* (London) (12 December), p. 17.
Another letter to the editor addressed to the governmental debate on the refinancing of the film industry. The undersigned support some vigorous proposals put forward by Leon Clore which would pull the industry out of its present economic slump.

437. "Preface," in *O Lucky Man!* by Lindsay Anderson and David Sherwin with songs by Alan Price. New York: Grove Press, pp. 7-9.
Anderson describes briefly how the script differs from the final film, and describes, also briefly, how the script came about as well as its composition. He explains that, with one exception, Alan Price's songs were written before the film was shot, and he makes some passing references to this film's connections with *If . . . .*

438. "Stripping the Veils Away." The *Times* (London) (21 April), p. 7.
A long interview with David Robinson about the making of *O Lucky Man!*, during which Anderson talks about the genesis of the film, what he feels the film is all about, and some of the problems of making it. Anderson explains and defends the ending, a rather controversial point with the critics.

1974

439. "Battle of the Film-Clip." The *Times* (London) (20 October), p. 17.
This is Anderson's response to an article by Peter Lennon who was criticizing United Artists for showing the clips from the film *Juggernaut* on one of the BBC film shows. Anderson explains that if anyone needs to be criticized it is the BBC for agreeing to show the clips in the first place. He also suggests that the BBC film programs could be produced more responsibly.

440. "Some Aspects of the Work of Humphrey Jennings," in *The Documentary Tradition: From Nanook to Woodstock*. Selected, arranged and introduced by Lewis Jacobs. New York: Hopkinson and Blake, pp. 236-243.

Reprint of "Only Connect: Some Aspects of the Work of Humphrey Jennings" (*see* no. 388).

Archival Sources

There is no one source of archival material on Lindsay Anderson. Neither his papers nor a complete collection of his films is housed in a single institution, but they are scattered in numerous places. Since he is a British director, the closest to such an archival source would undoubtedly be the British Film Institute. I list that institution here merely because it contains most of the periodicals to which Anderson contributed, and the background materials which were available to him in film.

441. The British Film Institute
281 Dean Street
London W1V 6AA
England

Distributors

442. British Film Institute
81 Dean Street
London, W1V 6AA
England
  Every Day Except Christmas
  O Dreamland
  This Sporting Life
  Thursday's Children

443. Contemporary Films (not yet distributed in United States)
55 Greek Street
London W1V 6DB
England
  The Singing Lesson (Raz Dwa Trzy)

444. Continental Films
100 North Gordon Street
Elk Grove Village, Ill. 60007
  This Sporting Life

445. Film Polski (35 mm only)
Foreign Trade Enterprise for Export and Import
Mazowiecka 6/8
P. O. Box 161
00950 Warsaw
Poland
  The Singing Lesson (Raz Dwa Trzy)

446. Grove Films
196 West Houston Street
New York, N.Y. 10014
  O Dreamland

447. The Library of Congress (non-circulating)
Prints and Photographs Division
Motion Picture Section
Washington, D.C. 20540

If...
In Celebration
O Lucky Man!
This Sporting Life

448. Ministry of Agriculture, Fisheries and Food
Tolworth Tower
Surbiton
Surrey KT6 7DX
England
Foot and Mouth

449. Museum of Modern Art
21 West 53rd Street
New York, N.Y. 10019
Every Day Except Christmas
Thursday's Children

450. National Coal Board
Hobart House
Grosvenor Place
London SW1X 1AE
England
Trunk Conveyor

451. National Society for the Prevention of Cruelty to Children
1 Riding House Street
London W1P 8AA
England
A Hundred Thousand Children
Green and Pleasant Land
Henry
The Children Upstairs

452. Paramount
9440 Santa Monica Boulevard
Los Angeles, Calif. 90025
If...

453. RBC Films
933 North La Brea Avenue
Los Angeles, Calif. 90038
In Celebration

454. United Artists (not distributed in United States)
Mortimer House
37 Mortimer Street
London W1
England
The White Bus

455. Warner Brothers
4000 Warner Boulevard
Burbank, Calif. 91503
O Lucky Man!

Index

149